Pathways for

Discovering the spir........, ... Iona Community in 28 days

Pathways for Pilgrims

Discovering the spirituality of the
Iona Community in 28 days

Chris King

wild goose
publications

www.**ionabooks**.com

Overseas distribution
Australia: Willow Connection Pty Ltd, Unit 4A, 3–9 Kenneth Road, Manly Vale, NSW 2093
New Zealand: Pleroma, Higginson Street, Otane 4170, Central Hawkes Bay
Canada: Bayard Distribution, 10 Lower Spadina Ave., Suite 400, Toronto,
Ontario M5V 2Z

Printed by Bell & Bain, Thornliebank, Glasgow

Contents

Introduction

Since its founding in 1938, the Iona Community has slowly emerged and evolved. At its heart is a spirituality of engagement: engagement with God, with the church and with the world. There is an intrinsic provisionality in the outworking of this as God's Spirit leads us to address the changing needs of the world.

George MacLeod, the founder of the Iona Community, came from a wealthy, aristocratic family which had produced five Moderators of the Church of Scotland. He had distinguished himself in World War I, yet his experience of being alongside soldiers from all walks of life changed him completely. It led him from a wealthy parish in Edinburgh to the poverty of Govan in Glasgow, and from being a military leader to a commitment to pacifism.

In Govan, during the Depression of the 1930s, he found skilled men with no hope of employment struggling to survive and to keep their self-worth. He became aware that the church had difficulty in reaching and touching the lives of the people in such communities. From this came the vision of rebuilding Iona Abbey, of unemployed craftsmen and trainee ministers sharing in a common life.

Initially the idea was for the ministers to stay for one or two summers, but the community spirit that developed led to the formation of the Iona Community. Thus what was a transient group of trainee ministers and workmen became a dispersed, permanent group, comprising mostly Church of Scotland clergy. This in time evolved to include lay people as well as ministers, women as well as men, all drawn from a wide range of denominations. There are now almost 300 Members living and working in all parts of Britain and overseas, coming together for plenary meetings and Community weeks on Iona, and meeting in small local Family Groups. They are held together by a five-fold Rule of: daily prayer and Bible reading; sharing and accounting for the use of resources, including money; planning and accounting for the use of time; action for justice and peace in society; and meeting with and accounting to each other.

The Community is first and foremost engaged with God. At the heart is the Members' daily devotional discipline and daily worship in Iona Abbey. George was a poet, and brought riches from many different Christian traditions to the Community. He drew on the Celtic heritage of Iona to revive the sense of mystery and awe. The worship he led, the prayers he crafted, and the sermons he preached inspired many who heard him. This gift for creative worship has become a continuing hallmark of the Community.

Engagement with God, however, also means engagement with the church. George deeply loved the church in all its diverse manifestations, and despite its brokenness, because the church is the Body of Christ. Many of the ministers in the Church Extensions that grew up in the new housing estates of the 1960s were Members of the

Community, bringing the spiritual vitality and concerns of the Community to parishes throughout Scotland. This has spread into the wider church family, stimulated in particular by the Wild Goose Resource Group and their ministry in developing new hymns and liturgies. And the Community's commitment to the renewal of the church continues, reflected in the active involvement of most Members in the life of their local church.

Finally, but just as centrally, the Community is engaged with the world. Rooted in a concern for healing, building community and supporting people in the journey of faith, there is a commitment to solidarity with those who are disadvantaged and to sharing in the creation of a just and peaceful world. This means not simply tackling the manifold examples of these wounds of humanity, but also working for social and political change. Faith and political action are inextricably combined.

Becoming a Member of the Community is not taken lightly. Usually people interested in joining become an Associate Member (there are around 1500 Associates worldwide, and about 1200 Friends) for a number of years, attending a Family Group and following some of the Rule. They then agree to undergo a two-year joining process, culminating in a 'hallowing service' of commitment and welcome.

The Community's administrative headquarters is in Glasgow, where its publishing house, Wild Goose Publications, the Wild Goose

Resource Group and its youth staff are also based. Over 100 guests each week (except during the winter months) visit the Community's three islands centres – the Abbey and MacLeod Centre on Iona, and the Camas Adventure Centre on Mull – where resident staff and volunteers carry out a ministry of hospitality. The life and activities of the centres reflect the Community's concerns and understanding of spirituality, providing guests with an experience of 'sharing the common life' through worship, discussion and relaxation together.

The Iona Community is almost 75 years old and is still evolving. It has grown and developed significantly but has remained faithful to its original vision and purpose. There are few founding documents and, although always grounded in prayer and wonderful worship, until recently little has been said specifically about its spirituality. Among the Community Members, there are different church backgrounds, and so different approaches to spirituality, although they all have a common core: the notion of 'engaged/integrated spirituality'.

Chris King

Week 1

Engaging with God

Day 1:

'Every blessed thing', by Norman Shanks

Community experience

Fundamental to the Iona Community's understanding of spirituality is the conviction that God's Spirit permeates the whole of life – 'every blessed thing', as George MacLeod, the Community's founder, said. God is thus to be discovered, encountered and experienced 'in the midst' of life – in the hurly-burly and daily routine of our lives, in and through our relationships, not just in tranquil moments and remote, beautiful places like Iona.

Iona is famously said to be 'a thin place' with no more than a tissue paper dividing earth from heaven; but, in one of his prayers, George MacLeod also said 'the whole earth cries glory'. And he told a wonderful story of a vandalised stained-glass window in an urban church, where a stone had removed the letter 'e' in the word 'highest' in the text 'Glory to God in the highest'. Thus, till unfortunately it was mended, it read 'Glory to God in the High St'! At least, George would say, the mended 'e' might have been contrived on a swivel so that in a high wind it would have been impossible to see which way it read.

So the Community's approach to spirituality, reflected in all its concerns and activities, expressed through the commitment of its

Members in their local situations, in the day-to-day life of the island centres on Iona and Mull and in the mainland programmes, does not distinguish between the sacred and the secular. Prayer and politics, work and worship are all of a piece.

Reflect quietly

The God of heaven is present on earth
in word and silence and sharing,
in face of doubt, in depth of faith,
in signs of love and caring.

(Wild Goose Resource Group, Iona Community)

Read this passage from scripture prayerfully

O Lord, you have searched me and known me. You know when I sit down and when I rise up; you discern my thoughts from far away …

Where can I go from your spirit? Or where can I flee from your presence? If I ascend to heaven, you are there; if I make my bed in Sheol, you are there. If I take the wings of the morning and settle at the farthest limits of the sea, even there your hand shall lead me, and your right hand shall hold me fast.

(Psalm 139:1–2, 7–10, NRSV)

Prayer

O Christ, the Master Carpenter,
who at the last, through wood and nails,
purchased our whole salvation,
wield well your tools in the workshop of your world,
so that we who come rough-hewn to your bench
may here be fashioned to a truer beauty of your hand.
We ask it for your own name's sake.

(*Iona Abbey Worship Book*)

Thoughts to ponder

When are you most aware of God being in 'every blessed thing' in
your day? When is it less easy to recognise God? What makes it difficult and what helps you to be aware?

Day 2:

Worship at the heart, by Jan Sutch Pickard

Prayer

The world belongs to God,
THE EARTH AND ALL ITS PEOPLE.
How good it is, how wonderful,
TO LIVE TOGETHER IN UNITY.
Love and faith come together,
JUSTICE AND PEACE JOIN HANDS.
If Christ's disciples keep silent
THESE STONES WOULD SHOUT ALOUD.
Open our lips, O God,
AND OUR MOUTHS SHALL PROCLAIM YOUR PRAISE.

(*Iona Abbey Worship Book*)

Community experience

These responses begin morning worship each weekday in the
Abbey on Iona. The ancient stones – some put in position in the
13th century, when the Abbey was first built, others 100 years ago,
during restoration – echo back the words. The congregation will be
a mixture of folk from different age groups, social backgrounds and

religious traditions, gathered as pilgrims to a remote and beautiful island to share a week of community life and reflection. Worship is at the heart of this, but it's not confined to what happens in the Abbey church. They have risen from the breakfast table to come into the church and will go out to share in housekeeping tasks in the Abbey and MacLeod Centre, before the day's discussions or craftwork or exploration of the island begin.

This pattern for the day is based on the experience of those who went out from morning worship in this church for 30 years of daily manual work, to rebuild not the Abbey church (that was already restored by then) but the cloister, chapter house, library, refectory, dormitories – what George MacLeod called 'the place of the common life'.

In the common life, everything is potentially worship – service to each other and an offering to God, a celebration of God's presence in the whole of life. At the end of the morning service, the congregation do not sit or kneel for a blessing, but remain standing for the closing responses, then walk out to their daily work. The blessing comes at the end of the evening worship – and in different ways throughout the day.

Read this passage from scripture prayerfully

When he reached the descent from the Mount of Olives, the whole company of his disciples in their joy began to sing aloud the praises of God for all the great things they had seen … Some Pharisees in the crowd said to him, 'Teacher, restrain your disciples.' He answered, 'I tell you, if my disciples are silent the stones will shout aloud.'

(Luke 19:37; 39–40, NEB)

Reflect quietly

Stand, poised for action. Feel your feet ready to walk into the world, your hands ready to work in a down-to-earth way for God, your lips ready to sing aloud.

Thoughts to ponder

In what ways do you try to keep worship at the heart of your life? What difference does it make if everything you do is seen as worship? What symbolic actions can remind you of that?

Day 3:

Healing and grace, by Norman Shanks

Community experience

The Iona Community's understanding of spirituality is founded on the belief that God's purpose for all is a life of wholeness, as expressed in the life and teaching of Jesus. So sharing in and facilitating the ministry of healing is an integral part of our Christian witness.

The Iona Prayer Circle, co-ordinated by one of the Members, is a fellowship of women and men, sponsors and intercessors all over the world, committed to praying for people and situations named on the monthly intercession list. In Iona Abbey every Tuesday evening there is a service of prayers for healing, during which, as requested, prayers are offered for particular people, places and situations. There is an opportunity, for those who wish, to receive or share in the ministry of the laying-on of hands – either for themselves or for another person or for a situation. This is a corporate and inclusive process: those leading the service are usually staff or Community Members; God's healing purpose and the promise of God's sustaining, trans- forming grace is for everyone, whether they come forward or remain seated in prayer and concern.

As confessed in one of the prayers used whenever Members gather and each weekday in the morning service on Iona, we are all broken people who stand in need of healing. With communities divided, nations at war, and the earth itself under threat, the world's healing too is a matter of urgent concern. Our prayers are complementary to the work of medicine and reconciliation initiatives that are also channels of God's transforming grace. We are not seeking in this ministry of healing to change God but to change the world, including ourselves. We pray hopefully and ready to be surprised, for we do not know when or how our prayers will be answered. We trust in the miracle and mystery of God's amazing grace.

Reflect quietly

We lay our broken world
in sorrow at your feet,
haunted by hunger, war and fear,
oppressed by power and hate …

We bring our broken selves,
confused and closed and tired;
then through your gift of healing grace
new purpose is inspired.

(From a hymn by Iona Community Member Anna Briggs)

Read this passage from scripture prayerfully

The Lord said to me, 'My grace is sufficient for all your needs, for my power is made perfect in weakness.' So, I will boast all the more gladly of my weaknesses, insults, hardships, persecutions and calamities for the sake of Christ; for wherever I am weak, then I am strong.

(2 Corinthians 12:9–10, NRSV, adapted)

Prayer

Before God, with the people of God,
I confess to my brokenness:
to the ways I wound my life,
the lives of others,
and the life of the world.

MAY GOD FORGIVE YOU, CHRIST RENEW YOU,
AND THE SPIRIT ENABLE YOU TO GROW IN LOVE.

(Prayer of confession from the morning service on Iona)

Thoughts to ponder

What do you find stimulates you to pray for God's healing grace for yourself and for the world? In what ways do you see God's grace active in yourself and the world?

Day 4:

Relevant worship, by Norman Shanks

Community experience

For worship to be relevant it should be effective, helpful and meaningful. For this to happen it must be contextual: flowing out of, engaging with, and relating to the needs and circumstances of those who are taking part and to the situation where it takes place. Being contextual is one of the primary characteristics of the worship of the Iona Community, reflecting our integrated understanding of spirituality. Thus many of the services led and shaped by Community Members, whether on Iona or elsewhere, seek to address current concerns and relate to specific activities: there have for instance been some memorable acts of worship at anti-nuclear weapons demonstrations at Faslane Naval Base.

It is also essential for the worship to enable communication to take place between God and the worshippers. Within the Community, the language and music of worship are given careful attention. Too easily the culture of worship can be exclusive – the words, concepts and music unintelligible and inaccessible to those unfamiliar with the culture.

This emphasis on the relevance of worship to particular issues and contexts is to be found not only in the services that take place on

Iona and when Members meet together elsewhere but also in the liturgies, songs and prayers prepared by Members for other occasions. Much of this material is published by Wild Goose Publications. It is also evident in the contribution Members make to the creation of worship in their own local congregations.

However, beyond and behind the commitment to make our liturgies relevant and accessible, and thus hospitable, there lies a deeper insight and conviction about the very nature of worship – that worship is everything we do, both inside and outside the church.

Reflect quietly

The excitement of Iona, when I first came, was discovering that not only was 'worship' not simply what religious people did in church, but that worship was everything that Christian disciples did and offered to God, and that this could be expressed in a style of living open and accessible to anyone, anywhere.

(John Harvey, Iona Community Member)

Read this passage from scripture prayerfully

Make a joyful noise to the Lord, all the earth. Worship the Lord with gladness; come into his presence with singing. Know that the Lord is God. It is he that made us, and we are his; we are his people, and the sheep of his pasture. Enter his gates with thanksgiving, and his courts with praise. Give thanks to him, bless his name. For the Lord is good; his steadfast love endures for ever, and his faithfulness to all generations.

(Psalm 100, NRSV)

Prayer

God in heaven,
your name is to be honoured.
May your new community of hope
be realised on earth as it is in heaven.
Give us today the essentials of life.
Release us from our wrongdoing
as we also release those who wrong us.
Do not test us beyond our enduring;
save us from all that is evil.
For you embrace justice, love and peace,
now and to the end of time.

(Modern version of the Lord's Prayer, Iona Community)

Thoughts to ponder

In what ways does relevant worship help you to engage with God? In what ways do you think local worship can become more relevant for everyone?

Day 5:

Participative worship, by Brian Woodcock

Community experience

I sat in the Abbey listening to a group of musicians prepare for the service. 'Worship is so creative here, and worshippers so responsive!' I thought. 'After three years on Iona, how will I cope with being an ordinary minister of an ordinary church again?'

But by good fortune we landed in Trinity, St Albans, which had been doing imaginative things with Sunday for a quarter of a century. Different teams took turns to organise group work for all ages, as on Iona – except they spent weeks rather than hours on it! After all those groundbreaking years, though, it was looking a bit tired and conventional. Some were longing for worship that was not interrupted by discussion or other unwelcome surprises! Why?

I happened to mention the Taizé Community, where teaching and group discussion is never mixed with the worship. I wondered whether worship there was a heart thing in its uninterrupted flow, whereas the other elements were more to do with the head.

'Well why not here?' someone asked. So now they split the morning into three parts. Worship first – readings and prayers led by members. Then 'time to share' – news and notices, coffee and socialising.

Finally, 'time to explore' - when the sermon or some other input, given from within the circle rather from the front, led to questions and thoughts from the congregation. That interactive conclusion was often the most rewarding, especially for me. Ministers no longer pretending to have all the answers. God's Word coming from everyone.

Read this passage from scripture prayerfully

Then afterward I will pour out my spirit on all flesh; your sons and your daughters shall prophesy, your old men shall dream dreams, and your young men shall see visions. Even on the male and female slaves, in those days, I will pour out my spirit.

(Joel 2:28–29, NRSV)

Reflect quietly

... It is time for the prayer of intercession, and the minister, in light-grey robe, asks, 'What prayers shall we offer God today?' There is a pause. Then a Puerto Rican on relief stands up: 'The landlord promised the Christian Action group he'd fix the plumbing on Betsie's apartment. Signed statement, too. We ought to thank God.' Another pause. Then twenty-two-year-old Josh is on his feet: 'Maybe we could pray for the families who'll be baptised next week?' Old Luigi rises, leaning heavily on his stick: 'Supposin' there was another gang fight like last night. I mean just supposin'. It'd be good if no one else got killed ...' The uneasy silence is broken by another voice, and another. Then: 'Let us pray.'

The pastor turns to the white communion table, looks up at the wooden cross that hangs on the deep-red wall, and then kneels to offer the prayers of the courageous, the strong, the rejected, the weak, the despised: those who, together, are discovering how social and spiritual chaos can be fought and overcome.

(From *Come Out the Wilderness* by Bruce Kenrick)

Prayer

Joined in community,
breaking your bread,
may we discover
gifts in each other,
willing to lead and be led.

(Brian Wren, from his hymn 'We are your people')

Thoughts to ponder

It is often said that you only get out of worship what you put in. How can more people be enabled to participate in worship? What sort of input from others do you find most helpful?

Day 6:

Prayer, by John Harvey

Community experience

We in the Community share a number of common experiences about prayer, apart from what we have been given through our own traditions. On Iona, we have learnt that prayer is both liturgical and free, and is fed from the Celtic, Benedictine and Reformed traditions. As we seek to keep the Rule, we learn how to be faithful in prayer for each other, for Associates, for the concerns of the Community, and for the concerns of the world church. In our Family Groups, we share our struggles and successes in prayer, and hopefully learn from each other. And in our daily life and work, we engage, with all people of faith, in prayer for our world, the church, and ourselves.

Some of the greatest gifts we have received are the prayers of George MacLeod. As well as leaving us some supreme public prayers, shot through with powerful poetic imagery, he taught us that prayer without action is as futile as action without prayer, and so formed us as a community founded on the action-reflection principle of 'see-judge-act', which underpins all our endeavours.

Reflect quietly

The most important thing is silence. Souls of deep prayer are souls of silence. We cannot place ourselves directly in God's presence without imposing upon ourselves interior and exterior silence. That is why we must accustom ourselves to stillness of the soul, of the eyes, of the tongue … The more we receive in our silent prayer, the more we can give in our active life. Silence gives us a new way of looking at everything. We need this silence in order to touch souls.

(Mother Teresa of Calcutta)

Read this passage from scripture prayerfully

(Jesus) told his next story to some who were complacently pleased with themselves over their moral performance and looked down their noses at the common people. 'Two men went up to the Temple to pray, one a Pharisee, the other a tax man. The Pharisee posed and prayed like this: "Oh, God, I thank you that I am not like other people – robbers, crooks, adulterers, or, heaven forbid, like this tax man. I fast twice a week and tithe on all my income."

'Meanwhile the tax man, slumped in the shadows, his face in his hands, not daring to look up, said, "God, give mercy. Forgive me, a sinner."'

Jesus commented, 'This tax man, not the other, went home made right with God. If you walk around with your nose in the air, you're going to end up flat on your face, but if you're contented to be simply yourself, you will become more than yourself.'

(Luke 18:9–14, from *The Message*)

Prayer

God, open to us today the sea of your mercy
and water us with full streams from the riches of your grace
and springs of your kindness.
Make us children of quietness and heirs of peace:
kindle in us the fire of your love;
strengthen our weakness by your power
and bind us closer to you and to each other.

(Prayer from the world church)

Thoughts to ponder

'Prayer is like waiting for the kingfisher. All you can do is be where he is likely to appear, and wait.'

(Ann Lewin, quoted by Sheila Cassidy in *The Tablet*)

What, for you, are the greatest challenges and the greatest rewards in your times of prayer?

Day 7:

Pilgrimage, by Brian Woodcock

Community experience

The weekly pilgrimage round the island is part of the life of the Community, and also of its welcome to all who come to Iona. A crowd of people setting off from the grounds of Iona Abbey for a challenging, reflective walk across the island. Pausing at particular places to prayerfully consider the history of the island or the course of their own lives. Finishing, appropriately, in the ancient graveyard chapel: place of resurrections and new beginnings. Finding they have come closer to fellow travellers, to the natural environment, to themselves; maybe to God. Pilgrimage is about individual quest and, sometimes painful, growth, within the context of shared humanity.

Coming to Iona is a pilgrimage in itself, of course. Pilgrims have been doing so for hundreds of years. And to other places of spiritual significance: Rome, Lourdes, Santiago de Compostela … Pilgrimage is certainly no invention of the Iona Community!

Nor of Christianity! Most faiths have pilgrimage traditions. I have seen countless groups of Hindu pilgrims trudging along South Indian roads: strange to Western eyes perhaps, yet humbling in their unashamed spirituality. I have heard a young Muslim tell a Lent group in Bristol how he accompanied his mother to Mecca even though he had no faith himself; and how, as he waited for her to complete the Hajj, something deep moved within him and turned his life around. You could have heard a pin drop as he spoke. We were hearing the parable of the prodigal.

Read this passage from scripture prayerfully

I was glad when they said to me,
'Let us go to the house of the Lord!'
Our feet are standing
within your gates, O Jerusalem.

Jerusalem – built as a city
that is bound firmly together.
To it the tribes go up,
the tribes of the Lord,
as it was decreed for Israel,
to give thanks to the name of the Lord.
For there the thrones of judgement were set up,
the thrones of the house of David.

(Psalm 122:1–5, NRSV)

Reflect quietly

I had been disappointed at first at the noisy ending to the pilgrimage, but as I sat, I became glad that it was this way. We need temples, churches and shrines, we need solitude and silence, but we need all these things to make us more aware of the mystery in which we are all living all the time … I had walked to Jerusalem to find Christ's peace. I left Jerusalem knowing that his peace is offered to us in every place and at every time. For his dwelling place is in our hearts.

(From *Walk to Jerusalem* by Gerard Hughes)

Prayer

God of the journey, as we travel on
alert us to the things that matter
and open our eyes to every sign of your presence.
Give us a sense of direction,
or at least a sense of purpose,
a sense of wonder,
a sense that, in everything,
you are walking with us step by step,
gently leading us to the heart of things.

Thoughts to ponder

In what way was the last journey of Jesus to Jerusalem a pilgrimage?
In what way is your life journey a pilgrimage?

Week 2

Engaging with the Church

Day 1:

'New ways to touch the hearts of all', by Norman Shanks

Community experience

The origins of the Community lie in a deep concern for the mission and renewal of the church. George MacLeod's experience in a deprived parish of Glasgow in the 1930s convinced him that the church was not reaching or touching the lives of ordinary people and that new approaches to training for mission and ministry were needed. Since then a commitment to 'rebuilding the common life' has been central to the Community's work – redefining social priorities, accompanying and supporting people on their journey, as well as embracing and developing new approaches to ministry and mission.

Over the years the Community has played a leading part in the development of several initiatives that have become part of the mainstream life of the churches, including industrial mission, training of lay people, house groups, campaigning for peace and justice. More recently, across the denominations, the worship of the churches has been enriched, through the work of the Wild Goose Resource Group and others, by the Community's innovative approach to liturgy and music, much of it available through the Community's publishing house, Wild Goose Publications.

The Community is not an alternative church but provides support for Members and others in their involvement with local congregations. The missionary challenge continues still in the contemporary context: how best to seek and explore 'new ways to touch the hearts of all', to share in the renewal of the church to enable it to embody the vision and values of God's kingdom and be an agent and channel of God's transforming grace.

Reflect quietly

The Church can only be a credible sacrament of salvation for the world when it displays to humanity a glimmer of God's imminent reign – a kingdom of reconciliation, peace and new life.

(David Bosch, from *Transforming Mission*)

And the one who was seated on the throne said, 'See, I am making all things new.' Also he said, 'Write this, for these words are trustworthy and true.'

(Revelation 21:5, NRSV)

Read this passage from scripture prayerfully

No one sews a piece of unshrunk cloth on an old cloak, for the patch pulls away from the cloak, and a worse tear is made. Neither is new wine put into old wineskins; otherwise, the skins burst, and the wine is spilled, and the skins are destroyed; but new wine is put into fresh wineskins, and so both are preserved.

(Matthew 9:16–17, NRSV)

Prayer

Ever-present God:
everything is still in your hands.
By the spirit of prophecy
you have awakened our souls to expectancy.
So let your resurrection light radiate all our worship
by the power of the Holy Spirit.
Help us to know ourselves
as women and men who have been made new.
By that same power inspire us to walk
even as he walked:
that going on our way in faith and gladness
we may come at last to those things
which eye has not seen nor ear heard
but which you have prepared for all them
that truly love you
from the beginning of the world.

(George MacLeod)

Thoughts to ponder

In what ways is God calling you, as part of your church, to be 'a sacrament of salvation' in your community – to display 'a kingdom of reconciliation, peace and new life'?

Day 2:

In the marketplace, by Norman Shanks

Community experience

George MacLeod famously drew attention to the significance of Jesus not dying in a cathedral between two candles but suffering a grisly death on a cross between two criminals on the rubbish-dump outside the city wall. And Ralph Morton, who served for many years with George as Deputy Leader of the Community, emphasised that the 'Iona experience' is 'for export': what matters is what you do with it when you get home.

The Community's incarnational theology affirms 'the beyond in our midst': alongside the mystery of transcendence, the importance of the humanity of God in Jesus. God's loving, transforming purpose embraces the whole world and the church is thus called to serve and witness in the places where people are and engage with the issues and needs that concern them. It is in the marketplace, in the hurly-burly of life, that God is to be discovered and encountered. In the early years the majority of Community Members worked in what were then called 'Church Extension parishes' (now urban priority areas) and overseas mission. Today Members work in a wide range of fields but the commitment to expressing and embodying the church's social engagement is as strong as ever.

Today it sometimes seems that shopping malls are the modern cathedrals and shopping is the focus, even the basic purpose of life. Pubs and clubs are the meeting places for music and dance, while football and rugby stadiums see the enthusiasm of the masses. The majority of people are no longer in the churches. The challenge for all Christians is to get out into the marketplace and raise the cross where the people are.

Reflect quietly

For the Church today the challenge is to find a way of focusing our attention *outside* the institution and to resist the temptation to become preoccupied with the insistent, internal demands for more money, new roofs, more clergy, more children in the Sunday school and more young families in the pews. Journeying out requires the capacity to rise above the anxiety associated with encountering and embracing a potentially overwhelming, outside world.

(Ann Morisy, from *Journeying Out*)

Read this passage from scripture prayerfully

Jesus Christ is the same yesterday and today and for ever … Let us then go to him outside the camp and bear the abuse he endured. For here we have no lasting city, but we are looking for the city that is to come.

(Hebrews 13:8, 13–14, NRSV)

Prayer

O Christ, you are within each of us.
It is not just the interior of these walls:
it is our own inner being you have renewed.
We are your temple not made with hands.
We are your body.
If every wall should crumble, and every church decay,
we are your habitation.
Nearer are you than breathing,
closer than hands and feet.
Ours are the eyes with which you, in the mystery,
look out with compassion on the world.

Take us outside, O Christ, outside holiness,
out to where soldiers curse and nations clash
at the crossroads of the world.
So shall this building continue to be justified.
We ask it for your own name's sake.
Amen

(George MacLeod, *Iona Abbey Worship Book*)

Thoughts to ponder

Where is the marketplace for you, where Jesus is calling you to stand with him? How do you feel about being 'outside holiness'?

Day 3:
A touching place, by Peter Millar

Community experience

We learn from history that when the Celtic monks were living on Iona, it was a place of welcome for – among many others – the stranger, the weary, the seeker and the penitent. And in welcoming those who came to its shores, the Columban monks were also welcoming God whose image lies deep within us all. As an Iona Community hymn says:

'The love of God comes close
where stands an open door
to let the stranger in,
to mingle rich and poor …'

(*Iona Abbey Worship Book*)

The modern Iona Community lives in a much changed world from that of our Celtic forebears. The fundamental social markers of our time are embedded in an astonishing human diversity. As never before we are globally connected in a web of cultural, social and religious differences; often vast differences which are frequently misunderstood. Given its conviction that this world in all of its plurality is the place of God's abiding, the Community continues to be a place which seeks to be as inclusive as possible of human diversity. In this task it has many failures – for the world is a complex place! In reaching out to all, the Community itself is on a journey of exploration and learning. To be 'a touching place' is perhaps one of the greatest challenges now facing the Community and is integral to its evolving spirituality.

Reflect quietly

Many of us in the world are slowly awakening to the acceptance of 'difference' … For some, this is an incredibly tough learning process; for others a vibrant expression of maturity within our human journeying. One thing is certain: 'Acceptance of difference' can never be a neutral experience for it demands a substantial rearranging of our emotional and spiritual resources.

(Peter Millar, from *Waymarks*)

Read this passage from scripture prayerfully

'Whoever welcomes you welcomes me, and whoever welcomes me welcomes the one who sent me. Whoever welcomes a prophet in the name of a prophet will receive a prophet's reward; and whoever welcomes a righteous person in the name of a righteous person will receive the reward of the righteous; and whoever gives even a cup of cold water to one of these little ones in the name of a disciple – truly

I tell you, none of these will lose their reward.'

(Matthew 10:40–42, NRSV)

Prayer

Lord of every human heart,
I ask you to speak to my heart,
to my mind:
to my imagination.

Help me to know that we are all different
and also all connected.
Enlarge my awareness.
Free me from prejudice.
Allow me to possess a mellow soul.
And in opening my heart to you,
may I also celebrate our shared human diversity
in all of its beauty, surprise and promise.

Thoughts to ponder

The chorus of John Bell's well-known hymn 'A touching place' ends with: 'Christ makes, with ourselves, a touching place', in particular for the lonely and the unloved. In what ways do you feel challenged by this?

Day 4:

God's frozen people, by Graeme Brown

Community experience

'God's frozen people' was how Deputy Leader Ralph Morton and Mark Gibbs described the laity in the middle of the last century, where the gifts of so many members – who could have contributed hugely to the life and mission of the church – were simply ignored. They challenged church leaders to recognise and encourage these people, and to make space for them to exercise their gifts.

These gifts, however, were to be exercised 'outside holiness' – within the workplace, in commerce and industry, in politics, in fact, in every sphere of daily life where Christian people sought to bring their faith to bear upon the world in which they lived. Their task was the rebuilding of the common life.

Ian Fraser called this process 'Reinventing Church', and for this task support and training was and is required. The Scottish Churches Open College was set up using dispersed learning to provide training for service in the world, enabling folk to find new confidence for their tasks. Groups were formed in parishes. Chaplains entered industries. Workers reflected together on their common task. Members of the Iona Community, like Ralph and Ian, were highly involved in these initiatives, and God's frozen people, far from remaining frozen, saw opportunities for servanthood well beyond church doors.

And so it was that our devotional lives were shaped by the circumstances of the world in which we lived and worked, or had no work.

Reflect quietly

[To be a Christian devoted to the rebuilding of the common life] 'is to undertake a hard and often uncertain pilgrimage. It is to struggle with a fog of ethical uncertainties, it is to face misunderstanding of both friend and critic, it is to face accusations of being "disloyal" and "worldly" on the one hand – and yet on the other to be thought oddly scrupulous, something of a "sucker", someone to be exploited. And this is our true vocation.'

(Ralph Morton and Mark Gibbs, from *God's Frozen People*)

Read this passage from scripture prayerfully

[The mind of the ploughman] is fixed on the furrows he traces and his evenings pass in fattening his heifers. So it is with every craft worker, toiling day and night ... All these put their trust in their hands and each is skilled at his own craft. A town could not be built without them, there would be no settling, no travelling ... They give solidity to the created world, while their prayer is concerned with what pertains to their trade.

(Ecclesiasticus 38:26, 35, 39, Jerusalem Bible)

Prayer

Christ has no body now on earth but yours,
no hands but yours,
no feet but yours.
Yours are the eyes
through which Christ's compassion
cares for the people of the world;
yours are the feet
with which Christ is to go about doing good;
yours are the hands
through which Christ now brings a blessing.

(St Teresa of Avila)

Thoughts to ponder

We all share our lives with other people, whether at home, at work, wherever. At what points does your experience of daily life shape your devotions? What is your vision of a world reshaped by God? And how are you involved in the reshaping?

Day 5:

Ecumenism, by Norman Shanks

Community experience

Since its beginnings the Iona Community, while initially related particularly to the Church of Scotland, has been open to people and influences from other Church traditions. Formally there are now links with all the major denominations in Britain and with the ecumenical bodies.

And similarly the Community's membership now comprises people from almost all the main Churches, although individual denominational loyalty is of little consequence alongside the shared commitment of Members to the Community's purpose, concerns and Rule. In recent years Community Members have played a leading part in ecumenical activities not only at local level, but also more widely: one Member was the first General Secretary of Action of Churches Together in Scotland (ACTS), another was Ecumenical Moderator at Milton Keynes, many have been involved in international ecumenical bodies and events.

The Community's ecumenical commitment stems from its understanding of spirituality as engagement and connectedness and its acceptance of the Gospel imperative to respond positively and creatively wherever there are signs of growth and hope as the kingdom breaks through. If the church is truly a sign and the first fruits of the unity of all things in Christ, then our divisions represent a betrayal of our nature and calling and, worse still, are an offence against God.

Reflect quietly

God's work is not about Presbyterianism, Catholicism, Methodism, Calvinism, Evangelicalism, Ecumenism, Anglicanism, Congregation-alism, or any of the other 'isms' to which so many of us seem so attached. It is about unity and reconciliation and peace so that the world may believe.

(Murdoch MacKenzie, Iona Community Member)

How trifling and unimportant are the things on which we differ compared with the wonder and glory of the faith we have in common, a faith which, if applied, would lead to the transformation of the whole of humanity in the twinkling of an eye.

(Roger Gray, Iona Community Member)

Read this passage from scripture prayerfully

Christ is our peace; in his flesh he has broken down the dividing wall, that is, the hostility between us ... So then you are no longer strangers and aliens, but you are citizens with the saints and also members of the household of God, built upon the foundation of the apostles and prophets, with Christ Jesus himself as the cornerstone. In him the whole structure is joined together and grows into a holy temple in the Lord; in whom you also are built together spiritually into a dwelling place for God.

(Ephesians 2:14, 19–22, NRSV, adapted)

Prayer

With the eye of a weaver,
you have chosen us –
such different threads –
to be gathered into unity
that the world might believe.

So may we not serve your purpose
unless we are open to each other;
not care for each other
unless we reflect your love;
nor dare to love like you
unless we are glad to accept
the cost and joy of discipleship,
as friends and followers of Jesus
in whose name we pray.
Amen

(Wild Goose Resource Group)

Thoughts to ponder

What, for you, are the most treasured gifts you have discovered in another denomination? What are the hardest challenges you feel we face in breaking down all that divides us?

Day 6:

Emerging Church, by Ruth Harvey

Community experience

The Iona Community was founded as a post-war movement for renewal within the wider church. With our roots in a reforming Church, we see ourselves as part of the continual reformation of God's emerging church. We understand 'church' as *'the Body of Christ in all its richness and worldwide diversity'* made up of *'followers of Christ who, in community, carry or hold the Word of the Gospel'* (from the Iona Community's 'Emerging Church Working Group report', September 2011).

As Members we meet in local Family Groups to account to each other for our five-fold Rule, while at the same time encouraging and supporting each other in our engagement with the local church. For many Members, belonging to the Iona Community frees us to become more engaged with the local church and its renewal. Some Members are involved in specific Fresh Expressions or Emerging Church projects locally and nationally.

It is this creative dynamic, between movement and institution, that is for many of us the hope for an emergent church reflecting fully God's kingdom on earth.

Reflect quietly

Heaven shall not wait for triumphant hallelujahs,
when earth has passed and we reach another shore:
Jesus is Lord in our present imperfection;
His power and love are for now and then for evermore.

(From a song by John Bell)

Read this passage from scripture prayerfully

They devoted themselves to the apostles' teaching and to the fellow-ship, to the breaking of bread and to prayer. Everyone was filled with awe, and many wonders and miraculous signs were done by the apostles. All the believers were together and had everything in common. Selling their possessions and goods, they gave to anyone as he had need. Every day they continued to meet together in the temple courts. They broke bread in their homes and ate together with glad and sincere hearts, praising God and enjoying the favour of all the people. And the Lord added to their number daily those who were being saved.

(Acts 2:42–47, NIV)

Prayer

O God, who gave to your servant Columba
the gifts of courage, faith and cheerfulness,
and sent people out from Iona
to carry the word of your gospel to every creature:
grant, we pray, a like spirit to your church,
even at this present time.
Further in all things the purpose of our community,
that hidden things may be revealed to us,
and new ways found to touch the lives of all.
May we preserve with each other sincere charity and peace,
and if it be your holy will,
grant that a place of your abiding be continued still
to be a sanctuary and a light.
Through Jesus Christ.
Amen

(Prayer of the Iona Community)

Thoughts to ponder

Reflect on the prayer above. What are the key phrases that resonate with you? What is the 'spirit' that you pray for in your church? What 'new ways' of being church, of being community, have touched your life? What does 'church' mean to you? What does it mean to you to be part of the emerging church today?

Day 7:

Provisionality, by Peter Millar

Community experience

'Provisionality' is a marker of our times, as it is within the life and witness of the Iona Community. In terms of our human future, much is uncertain. Some see this as a bleak prospect and dislike the fact that often we are unable to plan in detail for the future. There are multiple natural and man-made threats hanging over our lives, whether in the rich world or in that of the poor. For millions, it is not a choice but a necessity to 'take one day at a time'.

At the heart of the Community's spirituality is the belief that provisionality within our lives is a gift of God. A sign of God's Spirit in our midst. This means that life is a journey rather than an arrival, and that within that journey there will be many unknowns and uncertainties. Many risks, many setbacks and many failures will companion our joys, sorrows and hopes. The liturgies of the Community witness to this 'journeying in hope'.

The Community believes that Jesus was not advocating a thoughtless, improvident attitude to life, but was warning against a careworn, worried, fearful way of living each day. This way of seeing life is expressed in words we use in our daily Affirmation of Faith. We affirm as a Community, and with all creation: *'the unfolding purposes of*

God, forever at work in ourselves and the world'. In other words the ongoing journey under the guidance of God.

This understanding of the provisionality at the heart of life also challenges the Community to travel lightly and to not become static in its witness to the Gospel, whether on the island of Iona or in many parts of the world through the lives of its Members, Friends and Associates. It also means that the Community has to take risks and to not become downcast when it experiences failures. The task is to be both provisional and prophetic.

Reflect quietly

In welcoming the provisional into our daily living, we are not being reckless or otherworldly. Rather, we are recognising that not everything can be planned; that the next five months or five years may bring major changes, unsought for disappointments and sorrows, surprising joys and successes, painful struggles along with days of quiet waiting, bright sunshine and rich blessings.

Read this passage from scripture prayerfully

'This is why I tell you: do not be worried about the food and drink you need in order to stay alive, or about clothes for your body. After all, isn't life worth more than food? And isn't the body worth more than clothes? Look at the birds: they do not plant seeds, gather a harvest and put it in barns; yet your Father in heaven takes care of them!

Aren't you worth much more than birds? Can any of you live a bit longer by worrying about it?

'And why worry about clothes? Look how the wildflowers grow: they do not work or make clothes for themselves. But I tell you that not even King Solomon with all his wealth had clothes as beautiful as one of these flowers.'

(Matthew 6:25–29, GNB)

Prayer

This is Your day Lord
and I thank You for its freshness and possibility.
Help me to go through this day
not worrying too much about how it will work out,
but knowing that You hold me, and all of the world,
in Your hands.
And when evening comes
may my heart know
Your calm and Your light.

Thoughts to ponder

What concerns you most about being 'provisional and prophetic'? What do you find liberating and exciting about it? In what ways might being more provisional deepen your trust in and your relationship with God?

Week 3

Engaging with the world

Day 1:

Spirituality of engagement, by Norman Shanks

Community experience

Today, despite the onslaught of aggressive secularism, and the apparent indifference of the majority of people to the church, 'spirituality' is very much in vogue, sometimes in a form dressed up as pseudo 'Celtic', which is escapist, romantic and self-centred. However, the Celtic Church, from which George MacLeod drew inspiration, points us towards an approach to a grounded spirituality. As well as celebrating the beauty and tranquillity of God's creation, this is rooted in and grows through the common life, in encounters with God in the ups and downs and struggles of everyday life, in our relationships, and in addressing the issues of the day.

The Iona Community, while respectful of our Christian heritage, is more interested in the challenges of the present and future. In 2005 the Community agreed a formal statement of its vision and principles, which included the following: *'We are committed to the Gospel of Jesus Christ and to following where that leads, even into the unknown; engaged together, and with people of goodwill across the world, in acting, reflecting and praying for justice, peace and the integrity of creation; convinced that the inclusive community we seek must be embodied in the community we practise.'*

This understanding of spirituality, integrated and holistic – a spirituality of engagement rather than escape – stands in contrast to some of the more ethereal, nostalgic and self-indulgent approaches that are sometimes on offer these days, and is rooted solidly in scripture, most notably the well-known verse in Micah 6 (see below). It is in connectedness – with God, with others, with the world around us – that we discover our full spiritual identity (we are 'all together' within ourselves).

Reflect quietly

The Bible writers never use the word 'spirituality'; they concern themselves with the Holy Spirit, and what s/he is doing in the world; and seem to be more interested in the gifts of the Spirit, and in the fruits of the Spirit – love, joy, peace, patience, and so forth – than in a state of being called 'spirituality'. And so I have always been taught that to be 'spiritual' in the biblical sense was to be seen to be showing forth, in daily life, the fruits of the Spirit – and most particularly the one that, according to Paul, rises above them all – love.

(John Harvey, Iona Community Member)

Read this passage from scripture prayerfully

God has told you what is good; and what does the Lord require of you but to do justice, and to love kindness, and to walk humbly with your God?

(Micah 6:8, NRSV)

Prayer

God, our challenger and disturber, help us to confront
all that makes for death and despair
in our lives, our communities, our world.
May we never lose sight
of the possibility of transformation
and be continually surprised
by people who believe in one another.

(Joy Mead, Iona Community Member)

Thoughts to ponder

In what ways does worship, prayer and scripture inform and support your engagement with the issues of today? In what ways does your engagement inform your worship, prayer and reading of scripture? How can you develop and strengthen the reflective and active focuses of your life?

Day 2:

Faith and politics, by Norman Shanks

Community experience

Fortunately there seems more general acceptance today, than may have been the case in the past, that a concern for social well-being, and thus for political priorities, flows naturally and inevitably from Christian discipleship. The Gospel after all tells of God's promise and purpose of new life, the transformation of the world as well as the salvation of individual souls. Since its early days such matters have been an important part of the Iona Community's agenda. George MacLeod spoke out for years, a voice in the wilderness as it were, against nuclear weapons, a cause now close to the heart of all the mainstream Churches. Even into his nineties he was railing against the 'money boys', with prophetic insight into the problems of economic globalisation and international finance that now are all too familiar.

Many Community Members express their commitment to working for social and political change through political parties, campaigning organisations and church structures. Some are or have been local Councillors; others have played a leading part in the central social responsibility committees of their denomination, of public bodies and of organisations such as Christian Aid, Church Action on Poverty, CND, Scottish Churches Housing Action, and Positive

Action in Housing (for refugees and asylum seekers). Corporately the Community has shared in coalitions such as Stop the War, Make Poverty History, Scotland for Peace and Stop Climate Chaos.

Reflect quietly

Seek the welfare of the city where I have sent you into exile, and pray to the Lord on its behalf, for in its welfare you will find your welfare.

(Jeremiah 29:7, NRSV, adapted)

When I give food to the poor, they call me a saint. When I ask why are they poor, they call me a communist.

(Archbishop Helder Camara)

Religion without politics is irrelevant; politics without religion is dull and uninteresting.

(Raimundo Panikkar)

Read this passage from scripture prayerfully

Is not this the fast that I choose: to loose the bonds of injustice, to undo the thongs of the yoke, to let the oppressed go free, and to break every yoke? ... If you offer your food to the hungry and satisfy the needs of the afflicted, then your light shall rise in the darkness and your gloom be like the noonday. The Lord will guide you continually, and satisfy your needs in parched places, and make your bones strong; and you shall be like a watered garden, like a spring, whose waters never fail.

(Isaiah 58: 6, 10–11, NRSV)

Prayer

O God, you have set before us a great hope
that your kingdom will come on earth,
and have taught us to pray for its coming:
make us ready to thank you for the signs of its dawning,
and to pray and work for the perfect day
when your will shall be done on earth as it is in heaven.
In the name of Jesus Christ.
Amen

(*Iona Abbey Worship Book*)

Thoughts to ponder

Jesus came to change the world. In what ways are you being called to be politically active in order to change the world for good? What do you feel could help us be more effective?

Day 3:

Doing justice, by Jan Sutch Pickard

Community experience

The morning service in Iona Abbey is the basis for the 'Office' used when Members of the Community meet together. It contains these words:

Love and faith come together,
JUSTICE AND PEACE JOIN HANDS.
If Christ's disciples keep silent
THESE STONES WOULD SHOUT ALOUD.

Over the years Community Members have found themselves called to different ways of 'doing justice', and of speaking out. Areas of deep concern have included the unemployment, poverty and breakdown of community during the Depression of the 1930s – out of which the rebuilding project grew; the need for nuclear disarmament (seeing the use or threatened use of nuclear and other weapons of mass destruction as 'theologically and morally indefensible'), with demonstrations against the Polaris and then Trident submarines based in the West of Scotland; the injustices of apartheid in South Africa and of the Israeli occupation of Palestinian land; issues of environmental degradation, global warming, our dependence on oil and our need to find ways of living on this planet with integrity; marginalisation of the poor in our own society and the injustices suffered by asylum seekers. These concerns have led to concerted action by the Community. Many other causes have been taken up by individual Members, with passion and dogged determination.

Our Rule includes a Justice, Peace and Integrity of Creation Commitment, which begins with these statements:

We believe:

1. that the Gospel commands us to seek peace founded on justice and that costly reconciliation is at the heart of the Gospel.

2. that work for justice, peace and an equitable society is a matter of extreme urgency …

Altogether fourteen points – increasingly specific – are listed, and the second half of the list moves from what 'we believe' to what we – Members and Family Groups – will do.

Reflect quietly

What does 'costly reconciliation' mean to you? Where do you see it is needed? How do you see it happening, and through whom? Thank God for their commitment.

Read this passage from scripture prayerfully

Do not defraud your neighbour or rob him.
Do not hold back the wages of a hired man overnight.
Do not curse the deaf or put a stumbling-block in front of the blind,
but fear your God.
I am the Lord.
Do not pervert justice; do not show partiality to the poor or
favouritism to the great, but judge your neighbour fairly.

(Leviticus 19:13–15, NIV)

Prayer

God of Holy Justice,
you inflame our hearts with righteous anger,
and breathe upon us the gentleness of your peace.
Give us care for one another,
commitment to others,
and courage to challenge the powers of evil:
that we may comfort the afflicted,
and afflict the comfortable,
transforming our world's warring madness.
In the name of Jesus Christ,
who, riding on a donkey,
turned the world upside down.

(Jonathan Inkpin, a friend of the Iona Community in Australia)

Thoughts to ponder

'That we may comfort the afflicted, and afflict the comfortable'. In what ways do these words challenge you? What do you understand to be at the heart of the Gospel? How do you try to put your beliefs into action?

Day 4:

Peacemaking, by Jan Sutch Pickard

Community experience

At the end of the morning service in Iona Abbey the congregation gathered there each day use these responses:

This is the day that God has made;
WE WILL REJOICE AND BE GLAD IN IT.
We will not offer to God
OFFERINGS THAT COST US NOTHING.
Go in peace to love and to serve;
WE WILL SEEK PEACE AND PURSUE IT.

There is a daily commitment to seek peace. In a broken world there are many ways of 'seeking peace'. We need to begin with our relationships within our household – whether this is a nuclear family, our Family Group (the basic unit of the Community) or our local community. But some of us have been called to engage with larger issues – in their impact on other societies – though often it is most possible to be effective at a local level.

The Community already had insights into the Israel/Palestine situation through the ministry of several Members in the Scots Kirk in Jerusalem and in medical work. People like Colin Morton and Runa

Mackay have challenged fellow-Members to reflect on what a Christian response might be in this polarised situation: not to 'say peace, peace where there is no peace', but to work for peace with justice.

Read this passage from scripture prayerfully

Blessed are those who hunger and thirst for righteousness,
for they will be filled.
Blessed are the merciful,
for they will receive mercy.
Blessed are the pure in heart,
for they will see God.
Blessed are the peacemakers,
for they will be called children of God.

(Matthew 5:6–9, NRSV)

Reflect quietly

During the last decade several Members have served in the Ecumenical Accompaniment Programme in Palestine and Israel (EAPPI) in response to an invitation from Palestinian Christians to *'come and share our lives, see what is happening here – and then go back and tell your people'.* A non-violent presence in a potentially violent situation, whether watching what happens at checkpoints, walking with children to school or being present at demonstrations against the

Separation Barrier, Accompaniers give support, observe and report, and bear witness. Returning, they give an account of what they have seen, on the ground, to as many groups as possible. This could be called a feet-on-the-ground spirituality.

Prayer

God of those who hope against hope,
we pray for the land that we call Holy:
feeling the weight of suffering among its peoples,
neighbours in this narrow land,
separated by walls and fences and checkpoints,
and by history, religion and politics,
by oppression on one side, and fear on the other.
We pray for all who are bereaved and dispossessed,
for Israeli and Palestinian children born amid tension,
and yearn for peace with justice in their lifetime.

Thoughts to ponder

The stance of EAPPI is one of 'principled impartiality'. How easy do you think this is to sustain? Do you see other forms of 'accompaniment' happening nearer home?

Day 5:

Combating poverty, by John Harvey

Community experience

The Iona Community was born in Glasgow's Govan in the Depression years of the 1930s, when unemployment, and desperate poverty, were rife. George MacLeod's experiences there, ministering alongside people enduring terrible social conditions, placed the fight against poverty, and for social and economic justice, at the heart of the Community's life – and remains central to our witness today.

In the early years, when almost all Members were Church of Scotland ministers serving in deprived parishes, the battle against poverty centred on their activities in their places of work. Nowadays, when the Community membership is much more varied, combating poverty takes place in a whole variety of areas, including medicine, social work, politics, housing, and so on.

Central to our understanding of combating poverty are our convictions that prayer and politics cannot be separated; that economic, social and political justice are the fundamental Gospel requirements for a world free of poverty; and that the real experts in this campaign are the people who live in poverty themselves.

Reflect quietly

We believe:

… that work for justice, peace and an equitable society is a matter of extreme urgency …

…. that social and political action leading to justice for all people and encouraged by prayer and discussion is a vital work of the Church at all levels …

(from the Iona Community's Justice, Peace and Integrity of Creation Commitment)

Read this passage from scripture prayerfully

'Then the King will say to those on his right, "Enter, you who are blessed by my Father! Take what's coming to you in this kingdom. It's been ready for you since the world's foundation. And here's why:

I was hungry and you fed me,
I was thirsty and you gave me a drink,
I was homeless and you gave me a room,
I was shivering and you gave me clothes,
I was sick and you stopped to visit,
I was in prison and you came to me."

'Then those "sheep" are going to say, "Master, what are you talking about? When did we ever see you hungry and feed you, thirsty and give you a drink? And when did we ever see you sick or in prison and come to you?" Then the King will say, "I'm telling the solemn truth: Whenever you did one of these things to someone overlooked or ignored, that was me – you did it to me."'

(Matthew 25:34–40, *The Message*)

Prayer

God,
I have a simple prayer for the Church.
I pray that one day soon
I will be part of a church that when we pray for the poor,
we will pray for 'us' and not 'them'.
I pray for a Church that will not only have the courage
to work for the poor,
to struggle with the poor,
but will also be of the poor.
And I pray that one day
there will be no poor people in the Church
because there will be no poverty.
And I pray to you,
the God of miracles,

the God of the rich,
the God of the poor. Amen

(Martin Johnstone, Associate Member of the Iona Community)

Thoughts to ponder

'Of course the problem is not poverty, it's wealth. As long as we live in, and even applaud, a culture in which money is the bottom line, the top line and the front line, there will always be people having to live below the poverty line.'

(David Lunan, Commissioner of the Poverty Truth Commission)

Day 6:
Integrity of creation, by Neil Paynter

Community experience

All creation is sacred: because God is the Creator of all life.

Throughout the centuries, Churches and Christians have somehow come to view God's good creation as fallen, and have taken Genesis 1:26–28, where God gives humankind dominion over all created things, to mean domination.

Ghillean Prance, Science Director of the Eden Project, Cornwall, and a friend of the Iona Community who has led different creation-themed weeks on Iona, writes:

'Dominion, a word which has often been misunderstood, implies caretaking, to act as stewards of God's own purposes. It does not, in its biblical sense, imply the establishment of a competing reign … Dominion is not domination without justice, but rather responsible rule that does not exploit charges … A problem in the Western world has been that many Christian people have taken God's command of dominion as a divine authorisation to exploit the earth with no thought for the welfare of other cultures, other creatures, the landscape, the mineral resources, the oceans or the atmosphere. There is no doubt that persuasive and influential misinterpretations of Christian doctrine have led to environmental destruction and lack of respect for nature.'

In Genesis 2, another account of creation, human beings are made not in God's image but, like the plants and animals, from 'the dust of the earth' – the very topsoil (Genesis 2:7): and our role is not to rule, but to 'serve' (*avad*) creation (Genesis 2:15; 3:23).

Read this passage from scripture prayerfully

Then the Lord answered Job out of the whirlwind … 'Where were you when I laid the foundation of the earth? Tell me, if you have understanding. Who determined its measurements – surely you know! Or who stretched the line upon it? On what were its bases sunk, or who laid its cornerstone when the morning stars sang together and all the heavenly beings shouted for joy? …'

(Job 38:1, 4–7, NRSV)

Reflect quietly

The degradation and destruction of the environment – deforestation, erosion of topsoil, contamination of drinking water, pollution of cities – often has harsher, more immediate consequences for the poor than the insulated rich. Care for the planet is solidarity with the poor, for whom God has a bias. Living in right relationship with the earth is foundational to justice and peace for all.

Prayer

O God,
your fertile earth is slowly being stripped of its riches,
open our eyes to see.

O God,
your living waters are slowly being choked with chemicals,
open our eyes to see.

O God,
your clear air is slowly being filled with pollutants,
open our eyes to see.

O God,
your creatures are slowly dying and your people are suffering,
open our eyes to see.

God our maker, so move us by the wonder of your creation
that we repent and care more deeply.

So move us to grieve the loss of life
that we learn to walk with gentle footfall upon your world.

(From 'A Creation liturgy', *Iona Abbey Worship Book*)

Thoughts to ponder

In what ways could you consume less, pollute less, and tread more gently on God's good earth?

Day 7:

Solidarity with the oppressed, by Jan Sutch Pickard

Community experience

For over seventy years Members have been inspired by this ideal, as part of a radical understanding of Christian responsibility, linked to Liberation Theology. The rebuilding of the Abbey, with trainee ministers working side by side with and under the direction of unemployed craftsmen, was both a practical and a symbolic act of solidarity.

Today fewer Community Members are ordained ministers serving in areas of urban deprivation – and more are lay people (and ministers) with a deep social concern and a commitment to practical action. Even in a time of financial stringency, one part of the Community's budget which is constantly topped up is the Islands Access Fund, which enables people living in poverty, and on the margins of society, like asylum seekers, to come as guests to the centres on Iona. Even just for a week, sharing in the common life there, they contribute insights and energy from their own experience. Solidarity is not about patronage!

In the summer of 2011, Members of the Community gathered in Iona to reflect on the work of Church Action on Poverty, using testimonies and filmed interviews with those living on the edge. Inevitably this was a call to 'Close the Gap', to deeper engagement.

Reflect quietly

The Community's Justice, Peace and Integrity of Creation Commitment includes these words:

We believe …

… that everyone should have the quality and dignity of a full life that requires adequate physical, social and political opportunity, without the oppression of poverty, injustice and fear;

that social and political action leading to justice for all people and encouraged by prayer and discussion is a vital work of the Church at all levels …

How can we express real solidarity with the oppressed?

Read this passage from scripture prayerfully

To oppress the poor is to insult the creator.

(Proverbs 14:31, NEB)

Prayer

Sow seeds of justice in our hearts, Lord
and we will not let hope be snatched away from us
like the bird snatches seed from the path

Sow seeds of courage in our hearts, Lord
and we will not let fear or apathy
prevent our roots from growing deep
and keeping us strong

Sow seeds of persistence in our hearts, Lord
and we will not let the powerful or cynical
stand in our way
like the weeds that smother new shoots

Sow seeds of your kingdom in our hearts, Lord
and we will share our hope and work together

Sow seeds of your kingdom in our hearts, Lord
and we will delight in the harvest
that is enough for all.
Amen

(Rosie Venner/Student Christian Movement, for Church Action on
Poverty/Close the Gap)

Thoughts to ponder

The parables that Jesus told about the kingdom of God draw on many aspects of human life. In what ways do you find these parables are calls to solidarity?

Week 4

Engaging as community

Day 1:

Dispersed but always connected, by Norman Shanks

Community experience

The Iona Community is a dispersed community of almost 300 Members, with only a few on Iona at any time, and those changing frequently. Whereas the initial Community in 1938 was all-male and predominantly young, Presbyterian and Scottish, there are now almost as many Members living outside Scotland as in, and as many women as men; we are drawn from all the main denominations in Britain; the age range runs from 20s to 90s; and there are now more lay people than ministers.

What binds us together is our commitment to the Community's fundamental concerns for justice and peace and the renewal of church and society through the 'rebuilding of the common life', expressed through its incarnational theology and integrated spirituality, and above all through the five-fold Rule, which Members keep, and ten 'working principles' that were agreed more recently (relating to 'our passion, our movement, our centres, our publications, our environmental, social and economic values, participation, accountability, citizenship and partnership'). The Rule, explored in more detail in days 3 to 7 of this week, is based on the practice of mutual accountability (which takes place primarily through Members' local Family Groups). It serves both as a practical tool for personal priorities and spiritual growth and as a means of deepening our relationship with God and solidarity with one another.

Reflect quietly

We are not alone; we live in God's world.

We believe in God:
who has created and is creating,
who has come in Jesus,
the Word made flesh,
to reconcile and make all things new,
who works in us and others,
by the Spirit.
We trust in God.
We are called to be the church:
to celebrate God's presence,
to live with respect for creation,
to love and serve others,
to seek justice and resist evil,
to proclaim Jesus, crucified and risen,
our judge and our hope.
In life, in death, in life beyond death,
God is with us.

We are not alone.
Thanks be to God. Amen

(*Iona Abbey Worship Book*)

Read this passage from scripture prayerfully

As God's chosen ones, holy and beloved, clothe yourselves with compassion, kindness, humility, meekness and patience. Bear with one another and, if anyone has a complaint against another, forgive each other; just as the Lord has forgiven you, so you also must forgive. Above all, clothe yourselves with love, which binds everything together in perfect harmony. And let the peace of Christ rule in your hearts, to which indeed you were called in the one body.

(Colossians 3:12–15, NRSV)

Prayer

O God of all creation,
who has come to us in Jesus,
lead us in your way of love
and fill us with your Spirit.
Choose us
to bring good news to the poor,
to proclaim liberty to captives,

to bring sight to the blind
and set free the oppressed.
So shall your new creation come
and your will be done.

(*Iona Abbey Worship Book*)

Thoughts to ponder

What helps you keep a sense of real community with others, both those around you and those far away? What do you feel you gain from, and give to, those who are part of your community?

Day 2:
Iona, by Neil Paynter

Community experience

George MacLeod famously described Iona as 'a thin place. Only a tissue paper separating the material from the spiritual'. Iona has probably been thought of and experienced as a thin place – as a sacred place of pilgrimage – for millennia. St Columba likely came to the island (in 563 AD) because it was *already* a holy centre.

While Iona seems out on the edge of the world today, Columba's monastery was at the centre of a busy crossroads at the time – the sea being the 'highway' of the day. As Celtic scholar Ian Bradley has pointed out: *'The monastic life was far from being one of retreat and escape. Indeed, monasteries were almost certainly the busiest institutions in Celtic society, constantly teeming with people and fulfilling the roles of school, library, hospital, guest house, arts centre and mission station …'*

When George MacLeod came to Iona with a group ministers and craftsmen in 1938, to rebuild the Abbey buildings, he too was not seeking a retreat or an escape from the troubled world, or his self, romantic 'banishment to a lonely isle'. George's idea was for ministers and craftsmen to come to Iona to work together and learn from each other, and then go back to the city to help 'rebuild the common life' – rebuilding the Abbey, a sign and symbol to the world.

In search of the recovery and deepening of the common life in our own time, guests come to the Iona Community's centres today to experience a lively, diverse common life, and to take that vision back home to their own communities.

Reflect quietly

The Abbey community aims to be a group where people can feel safe – a sanctuary where they can open out, share their fears, reflect on their lives … Community life … grows fast as people wash dishes together, worship, engage in arts or music, and chat – at the dinner table, in the common room or Chapter House, on walks and out on the weekly pilgrimage round the island. During the course of the week people can expect to be affirmed – and challenged … Somehow, the Church at large must work at ways of restoring real community to its heart.

(Ron Ferguson, a former Leader of the Iona Community)

Read this passage from scripture prayerfully

Hear, O Lord, when I cry aloud,
be gracious to me and answer me!
'Come,' my heart says, 'seek his face!'
Your face, Lord, do I seek. Do not hide your face from me.

(Psalm 27:7–9, NRSV)

Prayer

Thank you for our time in community:
for deep, if fleeting, friendships,
for those conversations late at night,
for the vulnerable intensity lubricated by laughter,
for the freedom to serve others and to affirm ourselves
in the face of all that you know
and we know of our lives,
and we thank you for any sign that the churches
with which so many are disaffected
can yet be your body on earth in the community of creation.

(David Coleman, Iona Community Member)

Thoughts to ponder

'Our hearts are set on pilgrim roads not to satisfy ourselves with finding one holy place, not to romanticise this thin place, but to take this experience of the presence of the holy back into the thick of things …'

(Murphy Davis, a founding partner of the Open Door Community in Atlanta, Georgia, in a sermon in Iona Abbey)

Day 3:

The devotional discipline, by Norman Shanks

Community experience

The Community's Rule has evolved and been added to over the years; but daily personal prayer and Bible reading has been there since the beginning. It can give us helpful insights into the nature and purpose of God, the life and ministry of Jesus, and the continuing power and presence of God's Spirit. In the early years Members were required to spend at least half an hour on this early each day – and return a monthly record of due diligence! However, many Members today find that this is now the part of the Rule that is most difficult to keep.

At a practical level, patterns of contemporary life and domestic duties make this more difficult. At a deeper level, for many of us there is a continuing and challenging issue about the commitment to read specifically the Bible each day, aware that God speaks to us also through other writings on which we can equally helpfully reflect, and also concern at the approach that regards the words rather than the Word as absolute. Even more significantly perhaps there is the difficulty that, when our lives are full and busy, it is often our time for reflection and prayer that suffers: in our preoccupation with our next task we do not make sufficient time or find that we can get into the appropriate frame of mind to open ourselves to God within and around us.

And yet, paradoxically, we know from experience that our lives are enriched, our spirits are lifted when we do make good time for this reflection. Here too we see how, in line with the Community's integrated understanding of spirituality, the different parts of the Rule interact and depend on one another – the links between prayer and action and between the devotional and time disciplines.

Reflect quietly

Take, oh, take me as I am;
summon out what I shall be;
set your seal upon my heart
and live in me.

(From a song by John Bell)

Read this passage from scripture prayerfully

The wilderness and the dry land shall be glad, the desert shall rejoice and blossom; like the crocus it shall blossom abundantly and rejoice with joy and singing … The eyes of the blind shall be opened, and the ears of the deaf unstopped; then the lame shall leap like a deer, and the tongue of the speechless sing for joy. For waters shall break forth in the wilderness, and streams in the desert … A highway shall be there, and it shall be called the Holy Way; the unclean shall not travel on it, but it shall be for God's people; no traveller, not even fools, shall go astray.

(Isaiah 35:1, 5–6, 8, NRSV)

Prayer

God of life, of all life and each life,
I lay my life before you.
I give my life to you from whom nothing is hidden.
You are before me, God, you are behind;
you are around me, God, you are within.
You are in the light and in the darkness;
you know the secret thoughts of every heart.
I bring the faith that is in me and the doubt;
I bring the joy that is in me and the sorrow,
the knowledge and the ignorance,
the hope and the despair.
God of life, generous Spirit,
renew me with your life, this day and always.
Amen

(*Iona Abbey Worship Book*, adapted)

Thoughts to ponder

What devotional discipline have you developed? What do you find most helpful in keeping this discipline? What sort of other writings do you think God can speak through?

Day 4:

Accounting for resources, by Norman Shanks

Community experience

Since the 1940s Community Members have had an economic discipline that involved accounting to one another for the use of their money. Very recently, with increased concern about global climate change and the depletion of the earth's resources, we have begun to account to one another also for our 'carbon footprint', using a standard basis of calculation and seeking to achieve an annual 5% reduction, clearly an increasingly difficult goal.

George MacLeod famously said, 'only a demanding common task builds community'. Although it is in a sense almost counter-cultural to talk about money and our personal priorities and lifestyle in detail with one another in this way, the level of trust that develops within Members' local Family Groups is such that, although the calculations may be complicated, the experience is not nearly as threatening as it sounds. Rather the process is supportive – in terms of mutual respect and understanding – and through it we try to exercise good stewardship and affirm the worth of one another. The fact that most of us tithe (4% to the work of the Community and 6% to our local church and to voluntary organisations and campaigning bodies which we support and other good causes) – with allowance for special circumstances – is not perhaps so unusual; but we account to one another for the total use of our net income. The Gospel records the challenging words of Jesus, 'Where your treasure is, there your heart is also.' Money and its use is an intensely spiritual matter: in the use of resources the personal is public and ultimately political in its outworking and implications.

Reflect quietly

Power, money, resources are a gift, given for a time, to bring change – not to preserve the way things are, not to return to the way things were, but that we may receive and live and give.

(David Coleman, Iona Community Member)

What I kept I have lost. What I gave, that I have.

(Sydney Carter)

Read this passage from scripture prayerfully

Then someone came to him and said, 'Teacher, what good deed must I do to inherit eternal life?' … Jesus said to him, 'If you wish to be perfect, go, sell your possessions, and give the money to the poor, and you will have treasure in heaven; then come, follow me.' When the young man heard this word, he went away grieving, for he had many possessions. Then Jesus said to his disciples, 'Truly I tell you it will be hard for a rich person to enter the kingdom of heaven.'

(Matthew 19:16, 21–23, NRSV)

Prayer

O God, gladly we live and move and have our being in you.
Yet always in the midst of this creation-glory,
we see sin's shadow and feel death's darkness:
around us in the earth, sea and sky, the abuse of matter;
beside us in the broken, the hungry and the poor,
the betrayal of one another;
and often, deep within us, a striving against your Spirit.
O Trinity of love,
forgive us that we may forgive one another,
heal us that we may be people of healing,
and renew us that we may also be makers of peace.

(*Iona Abbey Worship Book*)

Thoughts to ponder

What are the resources you have, besides money: for example, talents, material goods ... What, for you, is most challenging in the concept of accounting for your use of your resources to others? What are, or do you think would be, the benefits of doing this?

Day 5:

Accounting for time, by Jan Sutch Pickard

Community experience

Part of the five-fold Rule is a commitment to planning and accounting for our use of time. Ron Ferguson, in *Chasing the Wild Goose*, explains it like this:

This obligation grew out of discussions on the abbey walls between ministers and craftsmen. The masons taunted the ministers with working only on Sundays.

'Oh no,' retorted God's anointed, 'we work eighteen hours a day.'

'When you go back to your parishes,' said the craftsmen, 'take a note of how long you actually work, and don't include things like reading the newspaper, and lying in bed pretending you are meditating.'

The ministers had to concede that, unlike the workmen, they didn't have to clock in and out and were accountable to no boss; this could easily lead to self-delusion and indulgence. On the other hand, a conscientious minister, faced with a never-ending demand, could work himself into an early grave. What was needed was accountability in the proper use of time.

The place where Members of the Community do this accounting now is in Family Groups. Such gatherings may include people with very different experiences of working and life-patterns: waged and unwaged, carers, volunteers, self-employed, unwillingly unemployed, retired, those 'taking time out'. But in every case planning to use time responsibly and creatively is important.

Reflect quietly

In the 'safe' place of the Family Group we ask each other:

'It seems as though you're working all the hours God sends. Do you really need the overtime?'

'Are you spending enough time with your family?'

'What are you trying to prove?'

'What are your priorities for the next few months?'

'What helps you to relax, re-creates you?'

In love, we can help each other to be more accountable for time, which is God's precious gift.

Read this passage from scripture prayerfully

For everything there is a season,
and a time for every matter under heaven:

a time to be born, and a time to die;

a time to plant, and a time to pluck up what is planted;
a time to kill, and a time to heal;
a time to break down, and a time to build up;
a time to weep, and a time to laugh;
a time to mourn, and a time to dance.

(Ecclesiastes 3:1–4, NRSV)

Prayer

Help me, in seizing the moment, to savour it;
not to give my time – your time – away recklessly:
however worthy the cause, however carefully I account,
however hard to say 'No',
without taking time to know your presence
in each given moment, and to live in it, and in you –
God of the here and now. Amen

(Jan Sutch Pickard in *Living the Rule*)

Thoughts to ponder

Do you experience time as a gift? When are you most aware of that?
To whom do you feel accountable for the way you use your time?
What would help you to be more accountable?

Day 6:

Commitment to action, by Jan Sutch Pickard

Community experience

The Community's Justice and Peace Commitment includes these words: 'We believe … that the use or threatened use of nuclear and other weapons of mass destruction is theologically and morally *indefensible* and that opposition to their existence is an *imperative* of the Christian faith.'

These are strong words: 'indefensible' … 'imperative'.

How does the Community live out this urgency?

We regularly, and often spectacularly, include within the worship at the Abbey, and beyond Iona, issues of peace, poverty, preservation of the earth. However, we are committed to taking more direct action whenever and wherever we feel called. This ranges from organising a week of discussions between peace activists and military men, being arrested during protest sit-ins – and having the wonderful experience of hearing hymns being joyfully sung within the cells of the police station – to being involved alongside the marginalised: immigrants in Glasgow, Palestinians under occupation, survivors in Bhopal. But at the root of much of the suffering and injustice are the policies and practices of governments and international business, and wherever we feel their policies are 'theologically and morally indefensible', then we feel it is imperative to challenge them.

Reflect quietly

We shared Communion at the gates of Faslane:
one of the places in a broken world
where breaking bread and drinking bitter wine
is most relevant.
We shared it to remember
security – not of barbed wire and missiles –
but of God's love
that risks all and gives life.
We shared, in a warm circle of believers.
But later, when we sat down on the cold road,
we found that the bread and the cup
had escaped, and were still out there in the crowd,
being shared, carefully, among people of all kinds:
this paradox
of pain and promise
being passed from hand to hand
in a broken world.

(Jan Sutch Pickard, from *Out of Iona*)

Read this passage from scripture prayerfully

'The Spirit of the Lord is upon me,
because he has anointed me
to bring good news to the poor.
He has sent me to proclaim release to the captives
and recovery of sight to the blind,
to let the oppressed go free,
to proclaim the year of the Lord's favour.'

(Luke 4:18–19, NRSV)

Prayer

We believe that God is present
in the darkness before dawn;
in the waiting and uncertainty
where fear and courage join hands,
conflict and caring link arms,
and the sun rises over barbed wire.
We believe in a with–us God
who sits down in our midst
to share our humanity.
We affirm a faith
that takes us beyond the safe place:

into action, into vulnerability,
and into the streets.
We commit ourselves to work for change
and put ourselves on the line;
to bear responsibility, take risks,
live powerfully and face humiliation;
to stand with those on the edge;
to choose life
and be used by the Spirit
for God's new community of hope.

(*Iona Abbey Worship Book*)

Thoughts to ponder

How would you express and affirm the faith that is in you? Could you join in the affirmation of faith above?

Day 7:

Meeting and sharing, by Norman Shanks

Community experience

Meetings are essential to the Community's life and where much of the mutual support and sharing takes place – in Members' plenary meetings on the mainland and on Iona, regular meetings of staff, committees, but above all in local Family Groups, as tellingly explained some years ago by a Member in the Community's magazine, *Coracle*:

'For me, the cutting edge of the Iona Community is sharpest in the Family Groups; in the sometimes uncomfortable but often wonderful reality of people meeting together to help each other follow the Rule and God's calling. They are challenging as well as cherishing. They show us the tremendous possibilities there are to respond to the challenge of God's Spirit. They are places to examine honestly the fullness of our own response … One of the greatest challenges of liberalism is learning to live in real, painful, Christlike, accepting love with people who disagree with us …

Family Groups are pointed because of the discipline they provide; the annual financial accounting and the accounting for use of time give our cuddly liberalism an effective edge. It's not enough to say how wonderful justice, peace, integrity of creation are. The way we live needs to show that they are values for our way of life and not just idealistic goals … Family Groups are where the theology of our Community becomes embodied ... Without my Family Group the Community would mean a nice place to go on holiday with interesting discussion and lively singing! The edge would be dull, blunted and ineffective.'

Reflect quietly

Community life is there to help us, not to flee from our deep wound, but to remain with the reality of love. It is there to help us believe that our illusions and egoism will gradually be healed if we become nourishment for others. We are in community for each other, so that all of us can grow and uncover our wound before the infinite, so that Jesus can manifest himself through it.

(Jean Vanier, Founder of L'Arche Community)

Read this passage from scripture prayerfully

So if anyone is in Christ, there is a new creation: everything old has passed away; see, everything has become new! All this is from God, who reconciled us to himself through Christ, and has given us the ministry of reconciliation; that is, in Christ God was reconciling the world to himself, not counting their trespasses against them, and entrusting the message of reconciliation to us. So we are ambassadors for Christ, since God is making his appeal through us; we entreat you on behalf of Christ, be reconciled to God.

(2 Corinthians 5:17–20, NRSV)

Prayer

Lord, make our hearts places of peace
and our minds harbours of tranquillity.
Sow in our souls true love for you
and for one another;
and root deeply within us
friendship and unity,
and concord with reverence.
So may we give peace to each other sincerely
and receive it beautifully.

(From the American Indian tradition)

Thoughts to ponder

The Family Groups provide loving support but also require demanding accountability for the way we live our lives. How important do you feel it is to belong to such a group? In what ways do you think church communities could provide this for everybody in the congregation?

The Rule of the Iona Community

The five-fold Rule calls Members to:

- Daily prayer and Bible reading

- Sharing and accounting for the use of our money

- Planning and accounting for the use of our time

- Action for justice and peace in society

- Meeting with and accounting to each other

The Justice, Peace and Integrity of Creation Commitment of the Iona Community

We believe:

1. that the Gospel commands us to seek peace founded on justice and that costly reconciliation is at the heart of the Gospel;

2. that work for justice, peace and an equitable society is a matter of extreme urgency;

3. that God has given us partnership as stewards of creation and that we have a responsibility to live in a right relationship with the whole of God's creation;

4. that, handled with integrity, creation can provide for the needs of all, but not for the greed which leads to injustice and inequality, and endangers life on earth;

5. that everyone should have the quality and dignity of a full life that requires adequate physical, social and political opportunity, without the oppression of poverty, injustice and fear;

6. that social and political action leading to justice for all people and encouraged by prayer and discussion is a vital work of the Church at all levels;

7. that the use or threatened use of nuclear and other weapons of mass destruction is theologically and morally indefensible and that opposition to their existence is an imperative of the Christian faith.

As Members and Family Groups we will:

8. engage in forms of political witness and action, prayerfully and thoughtfully, to promote just and peaceful social, political and economic structures;

9. work for a policy of renunciation by our own nations of all weapons of mass destruction and for the encouragement of other nations, individually or collectively, to do the same;

10. celebrate human diversity and actively work to combat discrimination on grounds of age, disability, mental well-being, differing ability, gender, colour, race, ethnic and cultural background, sexual orientation or religion;

11. work for the establishment of the United Nations Organisation as the principal organ of international reconciliation and security, in place of military alliances;

12. support and promote research and education into non-violent ways of achieving justice, peace and a sustainable global society;

13. work for reconciliation within and among nations by international sharing and exchange of experience and people, with particular concern for politically and economically oppressed nations.

14. act in solidarity with the victims of environmental injustice throughout the world, and support political and structural change in our own countries to reduce our over-consumption of resources.

Further reading

A Storehouse of Kingdom Things: Resources for the Faith Journey, Ian M. Fraser, Wild Goose Publications

A Story to Live By, Kathy Galloway, SPCK

An Iona Prayer Book, Peter Millar, SCM-Canterbury Press

Chasing the Wild Goose: The Story of the Iona Community, Ron Ferguson, Wild Goose Publications

Gathered and Scattered: Readings and Meditations from the Iona Community, Neil Paynter, Wild Goose Publications

George MacLeod: A Biography, Ron Ferguson, Wild Goose Publications

God's Frozen People, Ralph Morton and Mark Gibbs, Fontana, 1964

Hard Words for Interesting Times: Biblical Texts in Contemporary Contexts, John L. Bell, Wild Goose Publications

Iona Abbey Worship Book, Wild Goose Publications

Iona: God's Energy − the Vision and Spirituality of the Iona Community, Norman Shanks, Wild Goose Publications

Living a Countersign: From Iona to Basic Christian Communities, Ian M. Fraser, Wild Goose Publications

Living by the Rule: The Rule of the Iona Community, Kathy Galloway, Wild

Goose Publications

Living Letters of the Word: Readings and Meditations from the Iona Community, Neil Paynter, Wild Goose Publications

Out of Iona: Words from a Crossroads of the World, Jan Sutch Pickard

Outside the Safe Place: An Oral History of the Early Years of the Iona Community, Anne Muir, Wild Goose Publications

Reinventing Church: Insights from Small Christian Communities and Reflections on a Journey Among Them, Ian M. Fraser (may be found on the Internet), Ian M. Fraser

Reinventing Theology as the People's Work, Ian Fraser, Wild Goose Publications

States of Bliss and Yearning: The Marks and Means of Authentic Christian Spirituality, John L. Bell, Wild Goose Publications

The Iona Community & Sermon in Stone (DVD), Wild Goose Publications

The Whole Earth Shall Cry Glory: Iona Prayers, George MacLeod, Wild Goose Publications

This Is the Day: Readings and Meditations from the Iona Community, Neil Paynter, Wild Goose Publications

Waymarks: Signposts to Discovering God's Presence in the World, Peter Millar, SCM-Canterbury Press

Sources and acknowledgements

'The God of heaven is present on earth …' – from the song 'Heaven on earth', *Enemy of Apathy: Songs of the Passion and Resurrection of Jesus and the Coming of the Holy Spirit*, John L. Bell and Graham Maule, Wild Goose Publications, www.ionabooks.com, © 1988, 1990 WGRG, Iona Community, Glasgow G2 3DH, Scotland, www.wgrg.co.uk

'O Christ, the Master Carpenter …' – *Iona Abbey Worship Book*, Wild Goose Publications, www.ionabooks.com, © Iona Community

'The world belongs to God …' – *Iona Abbey Worship Book*, Wild Goose Publications, www.ionabooks.com

'We lay our broken world …' – From the song 'We lay our broken world', by Anna Briggs © Anna Briggs

'Before God, with the people of God …' – *Iona Abbey Worship Book*, Wild Goose Publications, www.ionabooks.com

'The excitement of Iona …' – John Harvey, from *This Is the Day: Readings and Meditations from the Iona Community*, Neil Paynter (ed), Wild Goose Publications, www.ionabooks.com

'God in heaven …' – From the Iona Community Members' Book

'It is time for the prayer of intercession …' – from *Come Out the Wilderness: the Story of the East Harlem Protestant Parish*, Bruce Kenrick, Harper & Brothers, 1962 (Bruce Kenrick was an early Member of the Iona Community, who founded the charity Shelter.)

'Joined in community …' – by Bren Wren, from the hymn 'We are your people, Lord, by your grace' © 1975 by Stainer & Bell Ltd

'The most important thing is silence …' – by Mother Teresa, from *Everything Starts from Prayer: Mother Teresa's Meditations on Spiritual Life for People of all Faiths*, White Cloud Press, 2000

'God, open to us …' – From the Iona Community Members' Book

'Prayer is like waiting for the kingfisher …' – Ann Lewin, quoted by Sheila Cassidy in an article in *The Tablet*, March 1992

'I had been disappointed at first at the noisy ending to the pilgrimage …' – by Gerard W Hughes, from *Walk to Jerusalem: In Search of Peace*, Darton, Longman & Todd Ltd, 1991

'The Church can only be a credible sacrament of salvation for the world when it displays to humanity a glimmer of God's imminent reign …' – by David Bosch, from *Transforming Mission: Paradigm Shifts in Theology of Mission*, Orbis, 1991

'Ever-present God: everything is still in your hands …' – From the Iona Community Members' Book

'For the church today the challenge is …' – by Ann Morisy, from *Journeying Out: A New Approach to Christian Mission*, Morehouse Publishing, 2004, p.3

'O Christ, you are within each of us …' – *Iona Abbey Worship Book*, Wild Goose Publications, www.ionabooks.com, © Iona Community

'The love of God comes close …' – from the song 'The love of God comes close', by John L. Bell and Graham Maule, *Enemy of Apathy: Songs of the Passion and Resurrection of Jesus and the Coming of the Holy Spirit*, John L. Bell and Graham Maule, Wild Goose Publications, www.ionabooks.com, © 1988, 1990 WGRG, Iona Community, Glasgow G2 3DH, Scotland, www.wgrg.co.uk

'Many of us in the world are slowly awakening to the acceptance of "difference" ...' – by Peter Millar, from *Waymarks: Signposts to Discovering God's Presence in the World*, Peter Millar, Canterbury Press, 2000, p.118

'... is to undertake a hard and often uncertain pilgrimage ...' – by Mark Gibbs and Ralph Morton, from *God's Frozen People*, Fontana, 1964

'God's work is not about Presbyterianism ...' – by Murdoch MacKenzie, *from Gathered and Scattered: Readings and Meditations from the Iona Community*, Neil Paynter (ed), Wild Goose Publications, 2007, www.ionabooks.com

'How trifling and unimportant are the things on which we differ ...' – by Roger Gray, from *Roger: An Extraordinary Peace Campaigner*, Helen Steven, Wild Goose Publications, 1990, www.ionabooks.com

'With the eye of a weaver ...' – by the Wild Goose Worship Group, from *Present on Earth: Worship Resources on the Life of Jesus*, Wild Goose Worship Group, Wild Goose Publications, 2004, www.ionabooks.com, © 2002 WGRG, Iona Community, Glasgow G2 3DH, Scotland, www.wgrg.co.uk

'Heaven shall not wait for triumphant hallelujahs ...' – from the song 'Heaven shall not wait', by John L. Bell and Graham Maule, from *Heaven Shall Not Wait*, Wild Goose Publications, 1987, www.ionabooks.com, © 1987, 1989, 2003 WGRG, Iona Community, Glasgow G2 3DH, Scotland, www.wgrg.co.uk

'O God, who gave to your servant Columba ...' – *Iona Abbey Worship Book*, Wild Goose Publications, www.ionabooks.com, © Iona Community

'The Bible writers never use the word "spirituality" ...' – by John Harvey, from *This Is the Day: Readings and Mediations from the Iona Community*, Neil Paynter (ed), Wild Goose Publications, 2002, www.ionabooks.com. Originally from *Coracle: the magazine of the Iona Community*

'God, our challenger and disturber …' – by Joy Mead, from the Iona Community Members' Book

'O God, you have set before us a great hope …' – *Iona Abbey Worship Book*, Wild Goose Publications, www.ionabooks.com

'God of Holy Justice …' – by Jonathan Inkpin, from *Holy Ground: Liturgies and Worship Resources for an Engaged Spirituality*, Helen Boothroyd and Neil Paynter (eds), Wild Goose Publications, 2005, www.ionabooks.com (Jonathan Inkpin is a friend of the Wellspring Community in Australia, a dispersed ecumenical community inspired by the Iona Community.)

'God, I have a simple prayer for the Church …' – by Martin Johnstone, from *Living Letters of the Word: Readings and Meditations from the Iona Community*, Neil Paynter (ed), Wild Goose Publications, 2012, www.ionabooks.com

'Of course the problem is not poverty, it's wealth …' – David Lunan, Poverty Truth Commission: www.povertytruthcommission.org

'Dominion, a word which has often been misunderstood, implies caretaking, to act as stewards of God's own purposes …' – by Ghillean Prance, from *Earth Under Threat: A Christian Perspective*, Ghillean Prance, 1996, Wild Goose Publications, www.ionabooks.com

'O God, your fertile earth is slowly being stripped of its riches …' – *Iona Abbey Worship Book*, Wild Goose Publications, www.ionabooks.com, © Iona Community

'Sow seeds of justice in our hearts, Lord …' – by Rosie Venner, from *Spark Newsletter: News from Church Action on Poverty*, Autumn 2011, www.church-poverty.org.uk. Used by permission of the Student Christian Movement

'We are not alone; we live in God's world …' – *Iona Abbey Worship Book*, Wild Goose Publications, www.ionabooks.com

'O God of all creation …' – *Iona Abbey Worship Book*, Wild Goose Publications, www.ionabooks.com

'The monastic life was far from being one of retreat and escape …' – by Ian Bradley, from *Columba: Pilgrim and Penitent*, Ian Bradley, Wild Goose Publications, 1998, www.ionabooks.com

'The Abbey community aims to be a group where people can feel safe …' – by Ron Ferguson, from *Chasing the Wild Goose: The Story of the Iona Community*, Ron Ferguson, Wild Goose Publications, 1998, www.ionabooks.com

'Thank you for our time in community …' – by David Coleman, from *The Pattern of Our Days: Liturgies and Resources for Worship from the Iona Community*, Kathy Galloway (ed), Wild Goose Publications, 1998 www.ionabooks.com

'Our hearts are set on pilgrim roads not to satisfy ourselves with finding one holy place …' – by Murphy Davis, from a sermon in Iona Abbey, from *Hospitality: the Newspaper of the Open Door Community* www.opendoorcommunity.org. (The Open Door Community is one of the Iona Community's sister communities.)

'Take, oh, take me as I am …' – by John L. Bell, from the chant 'Take, O, take me as I am', from *Come All You People: Shorter Songs for Worship*, John L. Bell, Wild Goose Publications, 1998, www.ionabooks.com, © 1994 WGRG, Iona Community, Glasgow G2 3DH, Scotland, www.wgrg.co.uk

'O God, gladly we live and move and have our being in you …' – *Iona Abbey Worship Book*, Wild Goose Publications, www.ionabooks.com

'This obligation grew out of discussions on the abbey walls ...' – by Ron Ferguson, from *Chasing the Wild Goose: The Story of the Iona Community*, Ron Ferguson, Wild Goose Publications, 1998, www.ionabooks.com

'Help me, in seizing the moment, to savour it ...' – by Jan Sutch Pickard, from *Living by the Rule: the Rule of the Iona Community*, Kathy Galloway, Wild Goose Publications, 2010, www.ionabooks.com

'We shared Communion at the gates of Faslane ...' – by Jan Sutch Pickard, from *Out of Iona: Words from a Crossroads of the World*, Jan Sutch Pickard, Wild Goose Publications, 2006, www.ionabooks.com

'We believe that God is present ...' – *Iona Abbey Worship Book*, Wild Goose Publications, www.ionabooks.com, © Iona Community

'For me, the cutting edge of the Iona Community is sharpest ...' – from *Coracle: the magazine of the Iona Community,* Issue 4/27, www.iona.org.uk

'Community life is there to help us, not to flee from our deep wound ...' – by Jean Vanier, from *Community and Growth*, Jean Vanier, Darton, Longman & Todd, 1989, p.330

'Lord, make our hearts places of peace and our minds harbours of tranquillity ...' – From *A Wee Worship Book: Fourth Incarnation*, Wild Goose Resource Group, Wild Goose Publications, 2004, www.ionabooks.com, © 2004 WGRG, Iona Community, Glasgow G2 3DH, Scotland, www.wgrg.co.uk

Contributors

Graeme Brown is a former Leader of the Iona Community. His present concerns are for equality justice in political life, the inclusion of homosexuals in Church life and peace with justice in Palestine/Israel.

John Harvey – I've been a Member of the Community since 1965, and have served as Warden of the Abbey and also as Leader. As a Church of Scotland minister, I've worked in parishes in areas of multiple deprivation in Scotland. I'm active in peace work, and also (now retired) in my local Glasgow church in areas of community development.

Ruth Harvey has been a Member of the Iona Community since 1994 and has lived/worked on Iona at various stages in her life. Among other things she is a trained Mediator through Place for Hope, and is passionate about the value of mediation and conflict resolution tools in everyday life, most particularly within our churches.

Chris King is a deaconess in the Church of Scotland. For over twenty years she has worked as a retreat leader at Smithstone House of Prayer, pioneering ecumenical work in spirituality on the west coast of Scotland. She is an experienced spiritual director, but prefers the term *anam cara* (soul friend). She has written a number of books on spirituality; these include a course on some of the main spiritualities of Christianity. This book is based on the set of course notes looking at the spirituality of the Iona Community. More information can be found at www.pathwaystogod.org.uk

Peter Millar is a former Warden of Iona Abbey and a Member of the Iona Community. He worked for many years in South India, with his wife, Dorothy.

Neil Paynter lived on Iona as part of the Iona Community's Resident Group for four years. He is Editor of *Coracle*, an editor with Wild Goose Publications and a Member of the Iona Community. He is a former night shelter worker.

Norman Shanks is a retired Church of Scotland minister with a long-standing commitment to working for social and political change. He was a career civil servant from 1964-79, convener of the Church of Scotland's Church and Nation Committee from 1988-92 and a member of the World Council of Churches Central Committee from 1998-2006. He was Leader of the Iona Community from 1995-2002, and is currently a member of the Greater Glasgow and Clyde Health Board.

Jan Sutch Pickard is a former Warden of Iona Abbey and a poet and storyteller, who has served as an Ecumenical Accompanier. She is a Member of the Iona Community.

Brian Woodcock is a Member of the Iona Community and a former Warden of its island centres. A retired United Reformed Church minister, he leads occasional retreats, offers a certain amount of work consultancy and is involved in interfaith work in Bristol.

ORMSKIRK WO1

TWO

WORLD WARS

N.H.S. HOSPITAL

CONTENTS

Area served by the original Ormskirk Union Workhouse [1]

INTRODUCTION

Ormskirk Hospital in the Southport and Ormskirk NHS Trust can trace its origins from the Workhouse Infirmary. The original William Culshaw buildings[2] of 1853 are now mostly demolished. A new hospital has been built on what was once farmland, leased from and later bought from Richard Rothwell and cultivated by the inmates. Little is left to imagine the size and complexity of its buildings.

It seems a pity that the history of the hospital could soon be forgotten.

I came to Ormskirk in 1963, and was immediately struck by the friendliness and good relationships between the staff at all levels within the hospital.

The older nurses would reminisce about the work they had done during World War Two, and many also remembered their work in the 1930s, - the years leading up to the implementation of the National Health Service. Many of their stories tallied, and although oral history is notoriously misleading, when the same story is told several times, there is probably some truth in it.

I then set out to try and corroborate this oral history with some documented contemporary records. It proved to be most frustrating.

There are no records in Ormskirk of the old County or Emergency Medical Hospital of the War years, either in the Hospital, postgraduate library, local Lancashire County Library or in the NHS Trust Offices in Southport.

I was told of a big bonfire, authorised by the Superintendent in the early 1960s, where many records, signboards, books and various artefacts from the Workhouse era were destroyed. I understand interested personnel acquired some of these items.

The Liverpool Record Office (Ormskirk was within the Liverpool Regional Hospital Health Authority) has no records relating to Ormskirk Hospital.

Neither the War Museum in Aldershot nor the main Territorial Army Centre in Liverpool has military records of activity in Ormskirk during World War Two (WW2). The Wellcome Institute of Medical History has no medical records for Ormskirk apart from a series of Medical Officer of Health (MOH) reports.[13] The Royal College of Nursing Archives were also unable to help. On the point of abandoning the search, it was suggested by Mona Duggan, author of the comprehensive *History of Ormskirk*,[33] that I should look in the Liverpool Medical Institution. There I found two lever arch files of correspondence labelled E.M.S. (Emergency Medical Service) 1939-1945.[3]

Though full of detailed administrative information, these letters give little idea of what it was like to live and work in time of war.

Having gleaned this information, I then went to the Lancashire Record Office in Preston. Here I found the Ormskirk Union Minute books recording the day-to-day activity of the committees within the workhouse, continuing beyond 1930 to the Public Assistance Institution (PAI) Minute Book up to 1946.[4]

The Master and Matron's Joint report of the PAI was also found.[5] This covered the 1930s, the period of the Second World War to 1946, and included references to the County / Emergency Hospital.

Neither of these documents had any information of the activities within the EMS apart from administrative details such as providing black-out curtaining material and some basic essential equipment such as beds. The number of admissions and discharges was also recorded.

In the same section of the Lancashire record office I found the records kept by the Ormskirk Urban District Council Army Social Welfare Committee.[6]

Next I visited the National Archives in Kew where I found details of the planned hutted wards and central administrative details.

Finally I visited the Imperial War Museum, London, where I consulted the 1940 diary of Lt Col SS Greaves, who had served on the Hospital Ship Atlantis.[7]

These are the texts which have corroborated the nurses' stories and which have formed the basis of my work.

It was wonderful to find that most of the stories I had heard were true, including some, which I had thought were a bit dubious!

Towards the end of my searches, I read an advertisement in the Ormskirk Advertiser, asking for information about the Military Hospital in Ormskirk. I had not realised that there was another war hospital in Ormskirk, this one based at Edge Hill College. This Military Hospital was staffed by military personnel and only took military patients. Information about the activity within the Military Hospital at Edge Hill has been quietly lost, and I was only able to find one report within the National Archives.[8]

It is quite a shock to us now to recognise that there were still 'sick poor' housed in the County buildings at the end of WW2 and not just one or two. Gradually these people were dispersed into the community. The last left in the early 1960s.

At the inception of the NHS, the hospital became known as Ormskirk and District General Hospital. The buildings were repeatedly modified to accommodate the ever-expanding needs of a modern health service, until at last they became obsolete and the new hospital was built.

Ormskirk played only a tiny part in the national provision of hospital care in the UK during WW2. For Ormskirk though, it meant the creation of a small but complete hospital service, replacing the inadequate Cottage Hospital.

If Ormskirk had not had the hutted wards and operating theatre brought with WW2, then at the inception of the NHS our local hospital might well be based at Greaves Hall[10] and there would only be out-patient and minor treatment facilities here. (As I write this now in 2007, how the wheel has turned full circle!)

The combined story makes fascinating reading. It also brings some pride, too, that Ormskirk Hospital made such a vital contribution to the relief of the sick and injured of two World Wars.

The nurses' stories make the whole history come to life.

Betty Underwood 2007

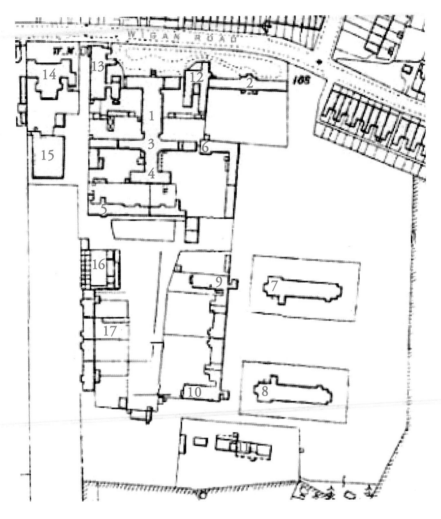

1 Priory /Stanley/ Nursery
2 Derby
3 Masters House
4 Dining Room / Chapel
5 Lathom
6 Laundry / Sewing Room
7 Female Pavilion
8 Male Pavilion
9 Female Infirmary
10 Male Infirmary
11 Children's Ward
12 Female Casual
13 Male Casual
14 Board of Guardians/Governors
15 Boiler House
16 Pigs
17 Workshops

Plan of workhouse buildings[11]

THE ORMSKIRK UNION WORKHOUSE

The 1834 Poor Law Acts allowed the union of several parishes to make a more uniform and economic provision for the poor.

The Ormskirk Union accommodated the poor of Altcar, Aughton, Hesketh with Becconsall, Rufford and Tarlton, Bickerstaffe, Birkdale, Bispham, Burscough, Downholland, Formby, Halsall, Lathom, Melling, North Meols, Ormskirk, Scarisbrick, Simonswood, Skelmersdale, and the Chapelries of Lydiate and Maghull. Each parish using the new union facilities had to pay the union costs of their poor.

Walton, Bootle, Litherland and West Derby also sent their poor when their own workhouse capacity was overstretched.

On the gravestones outside the Parish Church can be seen the evidence of such settlement, 'The Poor of Bootle', 'The Poor of Walton' etc.

The two-storey buildings were designed so that there was separate accommodation for able-bodied men and women. Elderly men and women lived alongside but separate from the younger men and women. There was a separate house for children and orphans. Each section of accommodation had its own separate exercise yard. Vagabonds and tramps stayed in single storey cellblocks, again separately accommodated in male and female units. The octagonal three-storey accommodation for the Workhouse Master and Mistress was situated in the centre, looking out over the whole.

The infirmary or 'County' was a two–storey, E-shaped building set away from the main workhouse area. The women's section, due to the fall of the land, also had a lower level that was used for maternity care. Again, the sexes were strictly segregated. There were separate wards for the acutely ill, but the long term sick and geriatrics shared the same wards. The sick children had a bungalow building to themselves. There was a play area outside for them.

The Pavilions were built later to house the mentally ill. The two-storey blocks for male and female occupants were not only separate but also had a high wall and railings around and between them.

In 1929, the management of the Poor Law Workhouse and Infirmary was transferred to the municipal Authorities, and was known thereafter as Ormskirk Public Assistance Institution (PAI) and the County Hospital or 'The County'. However the names 'Workhouse' and 'Union' were used interchangeably as the change over made little difference in the day-to-day working within the buildings, or in the eyes of the Ormskirk residents.

The whole complex was administered by a Board of Guardians.

Many staff appointed to the Institution remained there for their whole working lives. Some found their marriage partners there; others worked their way up from very junior positions to the most senior. It says a great deal about the working conditions, training opportunities, and atmosphere within the organisation.

The Union Minute Book of 1928/30 lists 52 guardians and Rev Ryan, 42 male and 10 female. The names listed here were given me at different times and may not be accurate.

1900+   Mr and Mrs Cain were Master and Mistress

Mrs Finch gave service for many years, eventually becoming Chairman of the Guardians. She lived in Fairfield House just behind the Institution site. Her daughter became the wife of Dr Haslam Fox.

Mrs George Blundell of High Wray was also a member.

Robert Taylor Senior was a Guardian who married Miss Masters, a nurse attendant from the female house. She worked her way up to become in charge of the female side of the Workhouse.

1920+   Sir Samuel Brighouse became Chairman of the Guardians.

Mr and Mrs Whittaker followed Mr and Mrs Cain as Master and Mistress of the workhouse. Mr Whittaker was ill for eight years and his wife took over most of the work. Annie Crossley was their maid.

Mr Beck started his career as an office boy to the Whittakers. In his free time he was a Scout leader. Every day he rode a motorcycle to work from West Derby. One day he had a serious road accident and had to spend twelve months on his back. He was nursed in the Cottage Hospital. Later he married Marie Bond from the Lodge. He worked very hard to become Deputy Master at the beginning of WW2 and then Master. At the inception of the NHS in 1948 he was appointed Hospital Superintendent.

Mr Bond and his wife lived-in at the Entrance Lodge. Mr Bond attended to the entrance gates which were kept closed by day and locked at night. He kept a Ledger of incoming and outgoing persons. The closing at night and registration of all who entered and left the premises continued till the 1960s.

1931   Mr and Mrs Alexander became the new Master and Matron of the Institution. They got rid of the old uniforms and introduced caps and aprons. They provided 'Butcher' dresses.

Workhouse Master and Matron's House

Mrs Taylor née Masters 1910-1920

Alice Whittingham 1891-1940

Unknown

Agnes Hardman in 1948

Sister Ducker

National Westminster Bank PLC

Entrance Lodge looking towards Wigan Road

They employed three relief attendants, a Lodge Porter and a gardener. It became apparent that the work of the Institution Matron was too much for one person, and so for the period of 1932-5 Miss Clark was appointed Matron of the 'County'. She in turn took on Annie Crossley as her maid. Mrs Alexander continued as Matron over the Female House.

1939/45 Mr and Mrs Oates became Master and Matron. They had as their Secretary Mr Nelson and Office boy H Woods.

Mr Woods became Chairman of the Regional Hospital Board, having worked his way up from the position of Office Boy.

Mr Robert Taylor followed Mr Woods. His father (also Robert) had been a Guardian many years previously.

Porters
G Houghton and H Ashcroft

Ambulance Driver
J Trafford

Derby House
Miss Whittingham
Miss Edna Cuddy looked after the inmates' children, the illegitimate and the abandoned.

Cook
Miss Edith Cuddy (ran the canteen where the cockroaches proliferated++!)

Children's Ward
Sister Richmond

Geriatrics
Sister Ducker on the male ward
Sister Rothwell on the female ward ('Twinkle Toes')

Psychiatric Ward
Chief Attendant, Mr Mallen

Finance
Mr Grant
Mr Ashton

Mr Hindle Robinson
Mr Stevens

Male House
Mr Bond

Female House
Miss Bamford
Mrs Taylor
Mrs Askins

Maternity
Sister Margerison

Gynaecology
Sister Crispin later Lawton

Theatre
Miss Morris
Sister Draper

Mr Stevens dealt with the money for the residents. The Finance office was in the Board of Guardians Building fronting on Wigan Road. Bank books were taken from the Geriatrics and these patients were allowed 7/6 (40p) per week, of which 5/6 (26p) was taken for the County Hospital and each patient received a florin 2/- (10p) for their own use.

Window cleaning was contracted to Howarth of Southport

Pork Butcher Holbert slaughtered the pigs and worked in the last shop of the coffin house on Railway Rd.

Barber Crompton, later Gilly Barnes

Mortician & Labour Master Mr Field

Engineer Sampson assisted by Kinloch

Storekeeper Edwards

Seamstress Miss Schofield

Farm Supervisor / Gardener Preece managed eight acres of land

Petrol Kinlochs' Garage

Works Clerk in the 1930s, Haskins

Laundry Supervisor Mrs Rimmer

Relieving Officers

Bill Postlethwaite	N Bottomley (Skelmersdale)
J Radclifffe	T Roberts
N C Lyon	

The Vicar of Ormskirk Parish Church was responsible for the spiritual needs of the inmates of the institution and for the children in the Industrial School. He was to provide burial facilities for the various parishes within the churchyard, baptise the babies, and provide spiritual instruction to the children and any adults requesting his advice.

In 1929/30, Dr Haslam Fox was appointed to the position of Medical Officer and Public Vaccinator to the Institution and to Skelmersdale for £200. He was responsible for the care of all the residents and staff within the Institution and Infirmary. All new Casuals (tramps) had to be vaccinated against smallpox. This brought him another £100 per year. He not only attended the in-patients in the Pavilions but also home visited and certified those mentally ill patients requiring in-patient care. Certification brought a further fee of a guinea (£1/1/- or £1.05p) for each case.

He performed daily ward rounds on all the wards including geriatrics and maternity. These were formal occasions and a nurse, who stood to attention, accompanied him all times. He conducted all post-mortems and completed all the coroner's office work.

Dr O'Regan, another GP in town, was appointed Poor Law Medical Officer. He held weekly out-patient surgeries in the institution. He issued Poor Law Cards to the destitute so that they could attend surgery or have a home visit. These cards were also valid in the out-patient clinics at the Cottage Hospital, and for any treatment prescribed there. He was Public Vaccinator for Burscough.

Dr Young was in General Practice in the town. He sold his practice to Dr Fox when he retired. Dr Fox then moved his practice to Ormskirk from Skelmersdale.

Each Guardian was a member of one or more of the eleven committees dealing with the efficient running of the Institution. The committees dealt with Finance, the House, the Farm, School visiting and Children's welfare, Boarding out of inmates placed in other institutions, Southport Relief and Casual Wards, Visiting, Salaries, General purposes, Buildings and Electricity, Contracts, and Stock taking.

Lancashire was always cost conscious, and kept expenditure to the minimum. The cost per head per week in 1927 was:-

	Shillings	Pence	New pence
Provisions	5	2	26
Clothing		9	4
Necessaries	4	10	25
Drugs		6	3
Total	11	5	59

The total number of inmates varied considerably too, but could be well in excess of 400. Families were segregated into the female (Stanley/Priory) and male (Lathom) houses and the older children were placed in Derby House.

Rarely, a family would be placed in the bungalows by the Works Department. The attendants responsible for the inmates were separate from the staff on the sick wards. They had a mainly supervisory capacity, little or no nursing experience, and wore a different uniform. Though the staff working on the Infirmary side might be asked to cover duties in the workhouse, it was never the other way round. New staff were interviewed and appointed by the Guardians after advertising in the Nursing Mirror and the Poor Law Officers' Journals.

The decision to admit a family to the workhouse was taken by the Relieving Officer. This was the last resort for people suffering severe poverty and was never intended to be an easy option for the needy indolent.

The Inmates were expected to work for their keep. Segregation of the sexes combined with the removal of children to separate accommodation was ruthlessly enforced. An authoritarian rule and supervision was imposed. The workhouse thus became a place to avoid if at all possible. Until very recently, elderly residents of this town still viewed admission to the hospital with a very real fear.

A collector or 'bailiff' had authority from the guardians to sell furniture and dispose of assets for the maintenance and defraying of costs for an inmate. The receiving officer only did this after very careful consideration and discussion of the report with the Guardians. Every effort was made to claim reimbursement of the inmate costs. For example, the husband of a lunatic woman was asked to pay 5/- per week for her care. Another person was admitted who had some personal effects. Of her money, 35/- was appropriated for costs, and another 6/- per week was allowed for spending.

The Board remained financially responsible for patients transferred to other hospitals or institutions such as Rainhill Lunatic Asylum or Nazareth House. Payments for lunatics in hospitals elsewhere cost £2/16/0 (£2.75p) per person per week.

In 1930, the Lunacy Account paid out:-

Rainhill Hospital	£352 19s 3d	(£352.90p)
Prestwich Hospital	£ 20 12s 6d	(£ 20.60p)
Winwick Hospital	£ 37 2s 6d	(£ 37.15p)
Whittingham Hospital	£155 0s 0d	(£155.00p)
Lancaster Moor Hospital	£153 6s 2d	(£153.30p)

Extra payment was given for the week including Christmas Day. Adults received 2/- (10p) each and children 1/- (5p) each. This extra relief was also given to those who were living in other institutions, schoolchildren and hospital patients chargeable to the Ormskirk Board. Extra relief was also granted similar to that allowed by the other workhouses in which they resided.

However, most of my story is about the thirties and forties, though I have related some relevant detail of earlier times for the description of work undertaken during the Great War (WW1). The admission, institution and nursing routines changed very little during this period. Most suitable able- bodied men and women were conscripted for war service in the 1940s when the number of casuals also diminished. A greater proportion of inmates were then geriatrics or people suffering mental health issues or learning difficulties.

The Workhouse Master and Mistress supervised the institution day-to-day activities. Living in the centre of the workhouse buildings, they were able to watch what was going on from their upper rooms. They had staff to supervise the fit, nurse the sick, deliver the babies, attend to the mentally ill, and to run the kitchens, laundry, sewing room, boiler houses, gardens, farm and estate.[5]

In 1930, a fire brigade was formed of Institution staff with the Superintendent and his Assistant in charge. The Superintendent was paid 5/- (25p), his assistant 3/6 (16p) and other staff 2/6 (11p). Ormskirk District Council provided a new four-inch main from the existing water supply in the road. Once the pump was repaired and working satisfactorily, the monthly fire drills worked well.

Other administrative duties were debated and approved or refused. Some examples are related here:-

Approximately 44 tons of slack (small waste coal) per year was bought for the furnaces in the boiler house.

A request for a telephone was received from the Receiving Officer for his private house. This was refused.

Hire of a car for 10/- (50p) was approved for him so that he was able to issue the outdoor relief while his motor bicycle was being repaired. This was necessary as his motorcycle was often out of action during the winter months.

Staff had to request permission to marry. Mr. Trafford, an ambulance driver and porter, had to apply several times before permission was eventually granted.

The cost of revarnishing and repairing the springs of the ambulance was also approved. Installation of electricity from Lancashire Power was approved in January 1930.

Board of Guardians and Finance Office

Water Tower

Outdoor relief

Outdoor relief was only available to those who needed temporary financial assistance in times of sickness or injury, or brief (hopefully) unemployment.

It is interesting to see the volume of work undertaken each month for the outdoor relief of the poor.

Persons in receipt of Outdoor Relief, Ormskirk

	Male	Female	Children	Total
1928/ a summer month	29	87	74	190
1928/ a winter month	38	88	107	233

Skelmersdale	Totals for the same two months	406/414
Southport	" "	864/991

The costs incurred for outdoor relief depended on the numbers of needy. This ranged in the years studied from £45/15/6 (£45.75p) to £47/19/0 (£47.90p). An additional 5/- (25p) was set aside to help those whose settlements should be elsewhere, as a temporary measure. All able-bodied men and women 'on the parish' had to work inside the institution grounds in return for their relief (a Community Task Force!). At first it was quite a problem to create jobs, but after 2 years of experimentation it was agreed the exercise had been most successful.

Ormskirk in the nineteenth century had had one of the highest infant mortality rates in the country.[12] There were many poor areas within the town - Aughton St, Chapel St, Green Lane, Hants Lane and Church St. All had old courts with houses constructed around a central yard and pump. The sanitation was primitive in the extreme with insufficient shared privies and overflowing middens; both of which sent their excesses through the yards and even into some of the houses. Too many people were crowded into the rooms, so that infection spread rapidly. Epidemics occurred and the death rate soared. Epidemics of cholera were the worst, and led to the authorities at last taking action. An improved sanitation system reduced the incidence of disease but did little to address the poverty of the inhabitants. It was mid twentieth century before the housing was totally renewed.

The 'clubs' - Tontines, Oddfellows, Rechabites etc - sometimes looked after the poor children. 'Going on the club' cost 2d per week for childcare, cover for adult hospital treatment and /or medicine, though the latter often cost a little more.

There was a Burial Club, initiated by Rev Wannop of Burscough and later taken over by Rev Russell. This was on a firm financial footing and was able to provide some relief for bereaved families.

Conditions inside the institution were basic, and the death register tells the story of the results of long-term deprivation.

The Town Ambulance, donated by Mr Blundell, was kept on Aughton St. This could carry six sitting cases or two stretcher cases. It was used to bring wounded convalescent soldiers to the Industrial School during WW1. I have no later reference to it.

The County Ambulance was kept at the rear of the hospital. The Rotary Club and Clucas' Seeds bought this ambulance. The first vehicle was a Ford 8. A porter or occasionally a senior member of staff such as Mr Beck would drive with a nurse in attendance to collect seriously ill patients. Occasionally two porters would be needed and the nurse would have to sit between them on the long front bench seat. Nurses were instructed to keep their skirts well down. The driver's hand manoeuvring the long gear stick could so easily explore her leg! Firemen were occasionally asked to drive. The journey could take a long time, as the distance travelled could be up to forty miles. The ambulance was also used to transfer surgical and maternity cases from the Cottage Hospital or County to Walton Hospital or Liverpool Infirmary, and very occasionally to Manchester.

I think the **Peoples' Ambulance** kept at the County Hospital[13iii] may have replaced this vehicle.

St. John's Ambulance was kept at Boundary St, Southport. This was used to bring vagrants into Ormskirk when the Southport facility was full. These people were usually alive with fleas, had lice in their hair and maggots in their sores. The ambulance had to be fumigated regularly.

The Fever Ambulance was kept at Green Lane Fever Hospital (later the Children's Hospital). This vehicle was not allowed out of Ormskirk except to take infectious adults to New Hall. It was painted yellow.

The Police used their own vehicle or ambulance to bring some of their 'clients' to the institution for basic medical care.

Vagabonds and Tramps were a feature of workhouse life. Some men and women preferred life on the road to institutional care. They had a route within the region, which brought them back to Ormskirk at infrequent intervals. Other workhouses were within 10 to 15 miles radius of each other. Marks were left to warn other travellers of poor food, harsh treatment, or hard work in certain houses!

There were two blocks of cells, one by the female accommodation and the other near the main entrance of the Institution. There were about 20 cells in each. The block by the Lodge entrance had shared access with the Police.

Each cell contained an iron bedstead, a straw-filled mattress and two grey blankets stitched with red wool. No linen was provided. The nurses' description of the cells matched exactly what is on display in Ripon.[14]

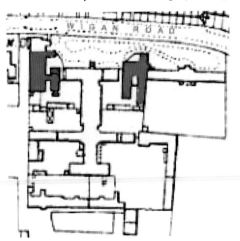

Those travellers requesting a bed had to be admitted by 6pm. No more than three nights were allowed. All personal belongings had to be handed over for stoving and then each person had to go for a bath. Many tried to hide cash on or in their persons, knowing that if found it would be appropriated for part payment of the care they received. Cleansing and delousing took place near the cells. Coarse soap was used for bathing and Oil of Sassafras as a shampoo. Sometimes Gilly Barnes, the hospital barber, would help with the cleaning of the new admissions.

Once they were clean, Dr Haslam Fox checked their health and then administered smallpox vaccination. Each person was then provided with some food, usually about 6oz (750gm) of boiled potatoes with some gravy and bread.

Next day a substantial breakfast of porridge (made in a huge boiler), half a loaf of bread, with cheese and a pint of tea was served in the canteen.

Pauper Delia Foy's route brought her back twice a year. She would add to her meagre income by reading the tea-leaves. She had an excellent reputation for accuracy, and would charge 3d a go!

Casual Ward, note the vents above each cell window

Lathom House

In return for their food and accommodation, the casuals were expected to do some work around the institution.

The female cellblock was closed down in the early stages of WW2 as the building was needed for other purposes. Some of the male cells were also closed in 1940 and used as a general store. However, in 1947, there were still some cells in use. The smell was abominable, and the whole building was closed soon afterwards and demolished.

Usually 350 – 400 casuals were boarded each year.

Once the cells were closed, vagrants continued to be admitted onto the general hospital wards so that their sores could be treated and their health assessed. The admission only lasted for a day or two. Occasionally they were admitted for Christmas when a warm bed and hot meals would be particularly welcome and gave them a break from the hardship of their normal lives. Certainly this was not uncommon when I did my Casualty stints in the 1960s and early 1970s.

Lathom House was the home of able-bodied men who were expected to work for their keep. They worked an eight-hour day, as did the women, with time regularly set aside for meals.

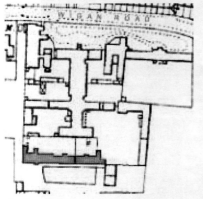

These inmates wheeled food to the wards, emptied bins, took the left-over food to the piggery and delivered post and papers. They worked in the greenhouse, in the grounds, brushing paths and planting the borders. They worked in the boiler house and in the Works or Engineers departments. Sometimes they chopped up railway sleepers into bundles of firewood, which were then sold.

Many of the fitter men worked on the farm. There were about 50 pigs, (? 12 -14) which were kept at the back of the works department. One year there was swine fever and the pigs had to be slaughtered and incinerated. The potato crop the following year was so fantastic that the Cambridge Institution Potato Testing people had to come and see!

(I am not sure if this refers to some pigs kept at Smithy Wood or the ones behind the Works department, or if it was the Potato Marketing Board of Ormskirk who were interested in the resultant magnificent crop.)

Lathom House, Elderly Men 1910-1920

The inmates also did the bulk of the painting and decorating work too. Casuals and men from the Pavilions would sometimes work in the same areas. They were supervised by a gardener and an attendant-in-charge. One or two were remembered in more detail; for example, Joe Foster brought bread and milk round to the wards and took messages. He also helped to bring fish from the station. Billy Bond bred canaries and did beautiful raffia work. He had been trained as a tailor before events occurred which led to his admission to the Institution.

Trusted men were allowed out to collect cans of petrol from Kinloch's Garage.

Inmates were occasionally allowed to go out for tea with the families of staff. The only other time they went out was when there had been a death. On these occasions, the small procession was lead by the labour master, and the coffin on a special handcart was escorted by 2-4 inmates to the Parish Church for burial.

The midday meal was served in the dining room next to the kitchen. This room was turned into a chapel on Sundays.

Geriatric men were housed at the end of Lathom House if they were capable of dressing and washing themselves. Many felt they were accepting 'charity' and some would try to do some chores to 'pay' for their care. There was a Mr Kirkby who used to shovel coke. Sadly, he eventually died doing it.

The men wore grey/white corduroy trousers, flat caps and grey shirts. Every article of clothing was labelled ORMSKIRK COUNTY HOSPITAL.

Each man was given 1oz (30gm) of tobacco every week.

This building was later used for medical staff housing, for the pharmacy, and as an administrative block.

The women living in **Stanley and Priory Houses** were mostly women capable of doing a full day's work. On admission many were in poor health because of malnutrition, continual childbearing or chronic disease. Most were infested with lice.

Some of the women had learning or physical disabilities which meant that they were unable to manage life on their own out in the community.

All the women were expected to work. Some worked on the chronic sick wards, others in the laundry or sewing room, for which they received a small personal allowance. Later they helped on the military wards for a further small remuneration. Some outside staff was also employed for kitchen cleaning and laundry supervision. All the women went to bed at 9pm. They slept in a long dormitory that had to be locked once they were all in bed.

Stanley House, Elderly Women 1910-1920

When on night duty, the attendant often felt as if she was a Prison Wardress and many other night staff didn't care for the work at all. She had a room off the main dormitory and rested there if she was on call. Night rounds were done every 2 hours to check that all was well. Older women were admitted into the adjoining section of the building. Some had become a burden to their families and as a result felt lonely and abandoned. They were not capable of working within the institution, but able to wash, dress and feed themselves. They lived in a day room off the large kitchen. They *just sat around in the day room and ate their meals*. These older women went to bed at 8pm in the long room over the day room, and were woken at 6.30am. Their washing was supervised on a rota basis. They made their own beds and tidied their area of the dormitory and then went down to the day room for 7.15am. Night Staff served breakfast and said Grace, and then wrote the night report. After breakfast the inmates cleared the tables and washed up.

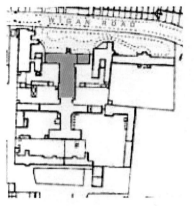

Unmarried pregnant women who had no suitable home, or who had been forced to leave home because of their condition would be admitted as inmates before the birth. They had to remain in the institution until the baby was adopted, fostered or taken into a Children's Home. They lived in a separate room from all the other women. They were despised and their lives were made even more difficult by the petty meanness that only women can devise. These expectant mothers were kept under close supervision all the time; otherwise once the baby was born they would run away. At 7.45am, they were taken across to work in the laundry. They were given only a very short time with their baby each day and were not allowed to feed or change it. Even under this strict if not harsh regime, once the women left the institution many were back again within a year. I was told of a woman who was not allowed back into the community after a second pregnancy until she was 56 years old.

In the 1930s, all the women were dressed in the same blue gingham dresses and pinafores. All clothing was stamped ORMSKIRK COUNTY HOSPITAL. All women received 4oz (120gm) of sweets per week.

These buildings were later used for administration purposes and for the medical Laboratory.

Priory House Babies 1910-1920

Pre School Children 1910-1920

The Nursery within Stanley and Priory Houses catered for children up to three years of age. These were not sick children. Some were there as part of a family admission, others because they were unwanted, because the mother was ill, or had died, or because their mother was unmarried. Some were admitted temporarily whilst their parents tried to find work.

Nursemaids did the feeds and nappy changes. Top-and-tail washes were done in the mornings before bottle feeds and light breakfast. If the mother was living in the workhouse, she could see the child for an hour before bedtime, but was not allowed to look after the child in any way.

The children were not supposed to be there for longer than six weeks. The Guardians who served on the Children's Committee made every effort to place the children for adoption in suitable homes. However, if the mother had prospects of being able to look after the child in the future, the Guardian would place them either in a foster home (not many such places were available) or into a children's home, usually Nazareth House, Layfield Homes, Olive Mount, Alder Hey, St Vincent's Children's Home or the Fazakerley Cottage Homes.

Derby House to Industrial School

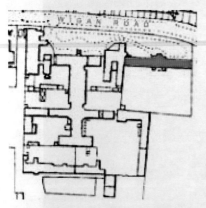

Derby House had been the 19th century home of the older children.

They had their dormitories and 'Charity' School there too. In 1886, a new residential Industrial school was built on the opposite side of Wigan Road (then Dicconson St) and the children were transferred across. The aim was to separate the children from the workhouse environment and give them a better moral training. The hope was that the school would 'depauperise' them, and enable them to take their place in society.

The reports now sound so patronising and self-congratulatory, but the conditions then were very bad, and the Guardians did what they thought would give the children a better start in life. The children were taught basic literacy complying with education regulations. In addition they were taught skills they could use in the future.

Derby House later Glendale Nurses' Home

The boys spent time cobbling, learning woodwork and farming, while the girls learned to bake and sew as well as learning household management.

They learned basic childcare too, and many went on to become a nursemaid or mother's help. All the children were placed in work at the age of 13. The Guardians went to considerable trouble to place each child in a suitable position. They would bring an unsatisfactory or unhappy child back to Ormskirk and find another more suitable situation for them.

By 1930, the empty Derby House was used as a Nurses' home and later renamed Glendale.

Industrial school to Convalescent Hospital in World War 1

At the outbreak of war in 1914 the Industrial Schools staff expressed their desire to support the war effort by accepting a lower salary. It was also noted that the schools could offer 50 beds for wounded soldiers, provided they had 4 hours notice. The sheer numbers of casualties had shocked the nation into wanting to do everything possible to help.

In February 1917, the military authorities finally offered to take and use the industrial schools for the reception of wounded soldiers.

The Guardians of the remaining 56 resident children made 'Alternative Arrangements', which meant that the children were placed in children's homes elsewhere and attended council schools from there. The Guardians still kept an interest in their welfare, and committee members visited from time to time. There are no records of what the children thought about being separated from friends and other family members.

The 'hospital' was duly opened in July 1917, as a subsidiary to Lord Derby's Red Cross Hospital in Warrington, based within the Lancashire County Lunatic Asylum at Winwick.[15]

Soldiers were admitted initially to Warrington for assessment and treatment. Those fit for transfer were brought by private cars (of Ormskirk people) or by ambulance to the school/ convalescent home/hospital.

The government only paid for essentials, and so the Board of Guardians set up appeals for donations of goods for the soldiers. Ormskirk rose to the occasion and provided many comforts, money and entertainments for the men. In November 1918, within 10 days of the end of war, an annexe of 54 beds was opened.

Convalescent patients continued to occupy the hospital until March 1919. The hospital was finally closed in April of the same year.

In 1920, the Guardians finally sold the school buildings to the Lancashire County Council Education Department. A new Secondary Modern School was opened within the building. This eventually became Cross Hall Comprehensive School which was finally demolished to make way for the new Ormskirk School.

THE INSTITUTION INFIRMARY / COUNTY HOSPITAL
(1930 to NHS)

The sick wards were built away from main poor law buildings, partly as a means of preventing the spread of infection, but also to separate the two areas.

The two-storey male and female blocks housed men and women suffering from acute and chronic illness, geriatrics, and a few surgical and orthopaedic cases. They were connected by another two-storey building.

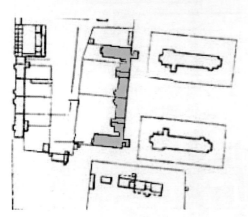

As far as possible the acute and chronic sick were kept apart, and as far as possible separate from the geriatric wards. The lack of effective treatments meant that recovery was slow, and depended on good nursing care. There was an opportunity for convalescent patients to go outside into the yards at the back of the wards.

The maternity and antenatal cases were housed on the lower ground floor of the female block with a tiny operating theatre.

Maternity was kept separate from the 'dirty' medical wards by separate access. There were no lifts, no dayrooms and minimal toilet facilities. A small Out-patients Department, later becoming Casualty and Antenatal clinic was created from the lower part of the central ward.

The two geriatric wards contained about 67 beds. They were staffed with six State Enrolled Nurses (SENs) and one Sister.

The **Children's Ward** was a single-storey unit with a veranda and a fenced play area outside.

The building consisted of three rooms; the babies were in the central section with toddlers in one side and older children on the other.

Because of the desperate housing conditions in some parts of the area covered by the institution, children were sometimes admitted with what could be relatively minor complaints, such as scabies.

Men's Ward - Infirmary 1910-1920

Women's Ward - Infirmary 1910-1920

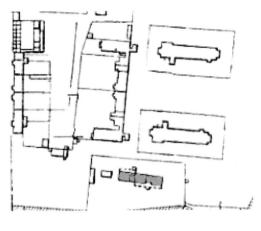

Sometimes there would be only one nurse on duty at night. In the middle ward there could be as many as twelve babies needing bottle-feeding. The only solution to this was to prop a bottle into each baby's mouth. Thankfully there were no mishaps.

The sluice was outside the ward.

Children with whooping cough and acute tuberculosis had their beds on the veranda.

Visiting was restricted to two people, preferably parents, for half an hour each day. NO children were allowed.

George Armstrong founder of the first children's dispensary in 1769 said 'if you take a sick child from its parents or its nurse you will break its heart immediately'.[16]

Admission procedure and normal working routines on the wards.

Nurses would go out in the ambulance to collect the patient for admission. This would be someone seriously ill and unable to make his or her own way into hospital.

They were all unable to afford to go to the Cottage Hospital. Many had no insurance scheme. Their families (if they had any) were either unwilling or unable to look after them, and often were unable to pay for their care. All the patient's property was taken and valued and then put in a safe place. This could then be sold in the future to defray the cost of his or her care, leaving each person with a small weekly allowance. Patients with acute illnesses such as pneumonia could be kept in hospital for up to six weeks, so the cost could be considerable.

The Public Health Medical Officer assessed the patients at home for geriatric long-term care before admission. The vast majority of them were both incontinent and bedfast and so were admitted to the Infirmary. Old people able to dress and feed themselves were admitted to the Institution. Most surgical cases were transferred to Walton or the Royal Infirmary in Liverpool. Some surgery was performed at the Cottage Hospital and the patient then returned to the County for recuperation.

The Operating Theatre in the County was barely adequate and difficult to make sterile. Occasionally Mr Walsh (gynaecologist) or Mr Heaney (surgeon) brought his instruments and operated. This was usually on a Sunday. There was no trained theatre Sister or staff. Nurses were called from the wards and had a chance of being on the call list if they were interested. This often led to them being on duty for extra long hours, as cases often occurred at times of staff change over.

All the Ward Sisters were State Registered Nurses (SRNs) and many also had a Midwifery qualification (SCM), none was young. Some had been trained at Walton Hospital or at the Royal Infirmary in Liverpool. Most were unmarried. They lived in at the hospital, and nursing was their life to the exclusion of much else. The ward sisters trained and provided experience for their juniors and expected obedience, a sense of duty and responsibility from their staff - words for the 40s and 50s but not for our current work situation.

The State Enrolled Nurses (SENs) worked in three month rotations of children's' work, male, female, geriatric and maternity. They also rotated day and night work. This system gave a good all-round training and also gave regular relief from the heavier tasks, and the more 'difficult' sisters.

The nurses took their meals at Blundell House within the hospital grounds, and £5 a month was deducted from their wages to cover meals and laundry even if living out. Knowles House on Burscough St was used as a Nurses Home. This was reported in the 1940s as being quite unsuitable for nurses' accommodation as there was very little toilet or bathroom provision, and that the building was in great need of repair.[17]

The work schedule was an arduous 57^1/$_2$ to 60 hours a week.

The Day staff duties were usually split, with some hours 'off' in the afternoon. Their day started before the night staff left. There was a staggered break for the nurses between 9 and 10am, and then an hour free for lunch.

There was one day off plus an afternoon for day staff. Night duty was by a rota of five nights on, sixth in at 11pm and then one off. Later this became five nights on, and one off one week and two off the next.

The night staff usually worked a twelve -hour shift from 8.30pm to 8.30 am. They saw to the patients' breakfasts at 7am before having their own breakfast at the hospital. This meant that any misdemeanours such as not emptying the pig-swill, broken thermometers etc would be found out before the nurses left the premises. Breakages had to be paid for by the nurse responsible, many of whom became adept at concealing such mishaps.

There was plenty of room for autocratic behaviour which led to the dismissal of more than one sister. Some sisters were known as 'ogres' yet these were usually also the most highly respected. They were the ones renowned for maintaining their high standards and for their training skills.

However there are always rogues willing to abuse the system.

An example of this was a sister who decreed that there should be no drinks after 5pm; in the hope of reducing the number of wet beds needing to be changed in the night. Cabbage was not served for a similar reason.

One member of staff was said to have cut a patient's hair out of spite, another filled her car with hospital soap!

One nurse even managed to take sheets home and when challenged she denied theft, saying she always brought them back each week for the laundry!

Interestingly, the nursing routines in the 1940s had changed little from those already in place on the sick wards of the 1930s. It was the advent of more efficacious treatments which enabled the patient turn-over to increase and the work load to diminish in later years.

Day duty began at 7.30am (8am for the Sisters) with bedpan rounds and washes. The beds were stripped and changed or remade while the patient sat in a chair.

Water bottles and glasses were washed and changed.

Locker tops were damp-dusted, enamel sputum pots were collected, emptied and sterilised (once a false eye was found in one!) and ward flowers were arranged with clean water.

Then the beds were pulled out one side at a time for floor cleaning, and the end casters were turned in to avoid anyone tripping.

There was teamwork for all the heavy lifting, e.g. lifting patients up and down stairs to Theatre or to the Labour wards in the days before lifts were installed, and in and out of bed. However, nurses suffered back strain on a regular basis.

Incontinent patients were cleaned 4-hourly with tow (cotton waste). They were then padded up with folded draw sheets. The routine for this was 3am, 8am, after lunch, after tea and at staff change. Extra supplies of linen were acquired (or hidden) so that their patients could be changed as soon as necessary.

Mondays and Tuesdays were bath days. Two nurses did the bathing, and a third made the beds. 'Backs' were washed, soaped until the soap disappeared, then after drying the skin, powder or cream was applied.

At one time, the skin was rubbed with surgical spirit; later this fell into disfavour. Any pressure sore was BAD NURSING. Ward sisters prided themselves that there were No Bedsores on Their Ward!

Sister did the drug rounds and supervised the dressings. Blood samples were taken to the mortuary, because the cool atmosphere there kept the samples fresh for the laboratory staff.

Doctors' ward rounds were usually done in the mornings, always with a nurse in attendance.

Four-hourly temperature, pulse and respiration rates were charted for every patient.

Books were kept to record nail cutting, baths, hair washing / cutting and weights at regular intervals for long stay patients.

A separate bowel book was kept too, and Cascaras were given out every Sunday night! After lunch the patients were expected to sleep or rest and read quietly unless the doctor was in attendance.

During this 'quiet' time, new patients were admitted and the nurses set up fresh trolleys, cleaned cupboards and sluices, scrubbed the steriliser, checked bedding and bagged laundry. They dried all the enamelware and put it away. Needles and syringes were put into trays of methylated spirit after boiling.

Bedpans, urinals, bowls and baths were all hand cleaned each day. A senior nurse was always in charge of this.

Surgical and Orthopaedic wards, which came with the advent of the hutted wards and operating theatre, needed more staff than the medical wards. There were 3-day skin preparations to do. The operative area would be shaved and washed with soap or ether/methylated spirits, the area was then covered with a sterile cloth and pre- and postoperative enemas were given. Dressings were hand-cut and cotton wool balls were made ready for autoclaving. Crepe bandages were returned from the laundry and rolled ready for reuse. The soldiers and long stay patients often helped with these tasks.

Dressings were renewed daily, indwelling catheters were released four-hourly, and any dirty linen was sluiced before being sent to the laundry. Many of the dressings and used swabs were washed and re-used.

Terminally ill patients were always kept in a bed near to sister's office, so that every care could be given.

Visitors (NO children) were allowed from 7 - 7.30pm each day, and at this time the nurses took a welcome break in the kitchen preparing the evening drinks.

Flowers were removed from the ward at night - and then it was hand-over time to the night staff. These were the days when all staff knew everything about every patient on their ward.

All the wards had to keep report books. These were completed at the end of each day and night shift. Each patient's progress (or lack of it) was recorded, along with treatment given and the plans for future care. These books had to be taken to Matron's office as soon as they were completed.

When Matron had finished with them, the books were collected and returned to the wards. An inmate was given this errand to do initially. In later years a junior nurse would be detailed for the task, and had to wait in a queue outside the office until her book was ready.

When a patient died, a nurse from the ward had to go down to the front office to make a statement (and receive 2/6). It just happened at one time that there were two women with the same name on a ward, one died, and was identified, but unfortunately the wrong relatives were informed, and insurance paid – before the other died 24 hours later and the mistake was recognised. One came from Southport and the other from Seaforth.[18]

The porters stoked the stoves except at night and at Christmas (when they were partying). This was always a contentious issue as the nurses often had to do it during the day. They thought they had enough to do without seeing to the stoves as well!

Matron did regular ward rounds with the senior nurses in attendance. The nurses had to secure their caps, check their stocking seams were straight, roll down their sleeves and put on their cuffs. Beds had to be straight and the counterpanes neat with envelope corners. Pillowcases had their open end away from the door. Matron would then talk to each patient, and because of the reports knew each one. Whilst she did the round, the junior nurses used to have a quick drink in the kitchen.

Heaven help the nurse whose black stockings were found drying on the steriliser!

The sick were quite well fed, often better than the nurses themselves.

Breakfast would consist of sausages rolled in flour, bacon, or boiled egg. The kitchen sent up porridge oats, cornflakes and bread, which the nurses toasted. Marmalade was set out and drinks were made.

Women's Ward 1940

Fresh Air at last for Spinal Carriage and Wheelchair users

The geriatrics tended to have a lighter meal, such as porridge, bread and butter with jam or marmalade and tea.

A morning break of Bovril in feeding cups and bread came at 11am. Later this became a tea, coffee, hot chocolate, or Horlicks round.

At about 11.30am, dinners arrived in electric trolleys from the kitchens. Food was plated up on the ground floor at noon, and the plates were carried upstairs, four at a time.

Typically, mince, potatoes and vegetables formed the main course. The vegetables were home grown. Rice, semolina or egg custard was offered for pudding. Fish was served on Fridays. Usually there was no choice of menu, though special diets were available for the diabetics and those with gastric ulcers.

Inmates helped feed those unable to feed themselves and then collected and washed the dishes. During the war, the convalescent soldiers sometimes undertook these duties.

Many of the inmates were real characters and were remembered with great affection by the nurses.

Dummie, as he was known, a deaf and dumb man, lived on the male ward. He knew more about the ward than a lot of the staff. He used to scold the nurses, collect bits of soap, and 'tell' Sister of everything that had happened when her back was turned.

Occasionally, young disabled patients were placed on the geriatric wards because there was no other more suitable accommodation available for them. Staff could become closely attached to them.

Eric was one of these. He was in a wicker spinal carriage. Sister Ducker would not allow the male nurses to bath him. He had virtually no arms or legs, but a normal trunk. His care was regarded as a punishment as he was very hard work, but it was always well done and Eric never had any pressure sores. Nurses occasionally took him out. When he had attacks of spasms he was massaged with zinc and castor oil cream.

Trixie (or Delia) was a young woman living on the geriatric ward who was paralysed from the neck down. She had been knocked off a wall by a speeding football. Like Eric, she lived in a spinal carriage. She was a lovely person and the nurses enjoyed taking her out to tea.

Though there were few effective treatments available, no easy antibiotics in those days, the best way of encouraging a return of health was with good nursing, good food, clean surroundings, fresh air and fun.

M&B 693 was the first sulphonamide available to treat bacterial infection. It first came into general use in 1943. Later streptomycin was introduced for serious infections, but because of its toxicity was soon restricted to the treatment of tuberculosis. It was almost at the end of the war before penicillin became readily available to the public.

Potassium Bromide Mixture, and paraldehyde were the only sedatives for the overactive and chloral was used for night sedation.

Great efforts were made to prevent cross infection from one patient to another.

Clean Orthopaedics cases were kept separate from Medical and General Surgical cases, and the maternity wards were kept separate from them all. This was such a serious issue that the maternity medical staff were not allowed to do Casualty sessions, and their nursing staff were not seconded to other wards.

Beds were kept clean, patients scrubbed, floors mopped, sluices kept running with strong antiseptic and utensils sterilised. The old buildings were not so easy to keep clean, and the blackout sometimes concealed HUGE cockroaches!

All this was exhausting work. During the war years there were staff shortages and a great deal of hard work to be done. The staff who related their stories to me universally enjoyed their experience

For all the hardship and heart–break, there was a sense of working to a common purpose and the job satisfaction was intense.

The Maternity Unit

Until 1930, most women had their babies at home, engaging a midwife or lying-in nurse. Some families opted for the comfort and extra care available in a maternity home. In this area most such deliveries were at Southport. The Christiana Hartley Maternity Home was opened in 1931,[19] replacing an earlier facility. Others chose the care offered by the Religious Sisters at Park House in Crosby.

However, where home conditions were unsuitable, due to lack of space or privacy, lack of running water, (never mind *hot* water) or dire poverty, mothers were advised to have their babies in the maternity unit at the 'County', where the inmates' babies were also born.

Maternity care was free until the 1930s, but a charge was then made of £4 for the 14-day stay. The relieving officer reduced the cost where necessary after interviewing needy mothers.

Mr Lawson Tate would come from Liverpool in the early days if there were problems. Later, difficult cases were taken to Liverpool for Sir Arthur Gemmell until Mr Walsh was appointed as visiting Obstetrician and Gynaecologist to Ormskirk.

In the early County days the maternity department was on the lower ground floor of the women's wards. There was a delivery room, tiny theatre and a lying-in ward.

When the EMS requisitioned the space for full operating theatre services in 1940, Sir Arthur Gemmell opened a new maternity unit on the upper floor of the central block, and the remainder of the geriatric female wards were used for lying-in. The chronic sick female inmates who had been on those wards were dispersed to other areas of the County. The provision of toilets and baths was grossly inadequate for the number of women nursed on each level.

Mr. Walsh was the first to use this new suite of four labour rooms, one of which could convert into an operating theatre. This room had an adjoining toilet, but no door. So much for antisepsis! The theatre table in the delivery room was not equipped for gynaecological procedures, but with manipulation, at the cost of stability, this could be achieved.

Most women needing surgery were taken to the new operating theatres. This entailed wheeling the patient on a trolley down the ramp outside the department and wheeling her along the road and round the corner. This was quite exciting if the case was a serious emergency or if the weather was inclement. The Antenatal clinic was moved to the upper floor with outside access up a steep staircase. Pre-eclampsia was then more easily diagnosed! Separate access kept outside 'germs' away from the lying-in and labour wards. Dr Haslam Fox was instrumental in improving the facilities in Ormskirk.

The two-week lying-in period was the only rest or 'holiday' many women got. Dr Fox was determined that the women should be treated 'like Queens'. They were to be given a better chance of regaining their health and hopefully do a better job of breast-feeding their babies.

This was achieved by improving the quality of care and by improving the quality of food provided. For example, chicken was served twice a week. This was at a time when the nurses themselves did not have that luxury. Even in the 1960s, it was common knowledge that maternity got the best food!

The meals were served on individual trays. The tray was set with a cloth, cutlery and stainless steel service, teapot, hot water jug, milk and sugar pots and cruet. A check serviette was neatly folded at the side.

Mothers were kept in bed for the first eight days. Then they were allowed to put their legs out of bed.

Personal hygiene was paramount, and with regular washing and swabbing, puerperal fever became a thing of the past.

Mothers had to lie face down for two hours each morning from 10am till 12noon. NO ONE was to disturb them. Even the nurses had to walk round the outside of the building!

The news got out, and women began to ask for delivery at Ormskirk.

Sister Margerison was a LARGE old style maternity ward sister. She was very strict and down to earth. There are tales of a coal fire and a rocking chair, but any tear or episiotomy were BAD midwifery to be ashamed of, as many a maternity nurse learned to her cost!

Mattresses were washed in carbolic solution between patients, bedding and napkins were sluiced and soiling was removed before dispatch to the laundry.

The babies were kept in the nursery. They only left it for feeds. This allowed the mother more time to rest.

The nurses made up little identity bracelets of pink or blue beads with the name of each child.

Downstairs Mat A babies were wheeled into the ward on a trolley for feeding. Laid crossways they would busily suck the head of the baby in front. The upstairs ward, Mat B, was a place where the more troublesome patients, unmarried mothers and antenatal women were sent. In truth this was for ease of evacuation in case of fire; the more active women were upstairs and the Caesarean patients and sick were downstairs. The babies were carried upstairs, (no lift in those days!) four at a time for feeding. The Liverpool Blitz of 1941 put an end to travelling to Southport or Liverpool for maternity care, and for the remainder of the War years most babies were born at home or in Ormskirk County hospital.

The Male and Female Pavilions.

The old map of Ormskirk dated 1890 shows the Workhouse and Infirmary buildings, but no separate psychiatric block. However, the census of 1881 lists both male and female lunatic attendants. The next map of 1908 shows one Pavilion block; the second block, which is the mirror image of the first, was built soon afterwards.

Each of the two buildings had two floors. A high wall topped with iron railings surrounded the wards. The gates were kept locked.

To gain admission, a bell at the gate would summon an attendant who had a large bunch of keys and who would then open the gates and the ward door. The clinking of the keys was a well-remembered feature of mental hospital life.

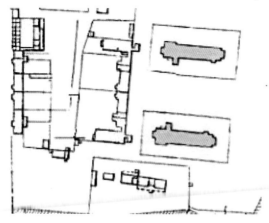

In the early days, mental illness and learning difficulties were not differentiated. The 1881 census lists 32 inmates as 'imbecile'. Later, of course, after the Pavilions were built, psychiatry became a specialty of its own and the different kinds of mental illness were recognised and separated from the various learning difficulties. Patients were admitted from the general community, not just the poor.

Those wanting private facilities could go to Formby or Haydock.

Some patients were admitted on a voluntary basis.

Compulsory admission was arranged by the Relieving Officer and the Medical Officer, Dr Haslam Fox. They visited the sick person at home to make an assessment and sign the certificate required for admission. This certified the person as 'insane'. Patients were admitted on a 3-day order, and if they remained violent after this period they would be sent on to one of the larger county lunatic asylums in Rainhill, Lancaster or Winwick.

The Guardians appointed special asylum visitors to visit those transferred to other institutions and encourage a speedy return. It was cheaper to keep the patients in Ormskirk if at all possible.

Psychiatric Ward

Interior of a Padded Cell

Though the buildings have changed very little externally since they were built, the internal arrangements were vastly improved by the addition of privacy curtains between the beds and a new toilet block. Much later, the male and female wards were linked with day rooms and the modern Scarisbrick centre was built.

The beds were crowded together in the upstairs wards, leaving the ground floors vacant for daytime activity and meals. The sexes were strictly segregated. Each unit had at least one padded cell for the isolation of noisy or violently aggressive patients. These 'pads' had bars over the windows; the bed was an integral part of the room, built solidly into the floor and wall, and fitted with a thin flock mattress. The walls and door were covered with a padding of flock covered with ticking so that noise was dulled and patients protected from self-harm through head-banging or violent activity. The padding also muted the noise from the general ward and added to the calm and quiet of the room.

A new padded cell was made in 1928 at the cost of £225/10/6 (£225.50p).

There was little scope for medical management. Chloral, paraldehyde, bromide mixture and laudanum (an opiate) were the only available sedatives.

Largactil (initially promoted for taming tigers!) was first used as a sedative in the 1950s. Environmental control through seclusion and a strict observance of routine was used with benefit to some of the more nervous or anxious patients. Work within the institution was also regarded as therapeutic.

Chronic long–term and institutionalised patients were usually incontinent. They wore special 'padded' suits, rather like a boiler suit. These had buttons at the back to allow changing of protective underwear.

Trusted patients were allowed out of the enclosure. Men under the supervision of an attendant would help on the farm, do painting and decorating and help with the general maintenance of the grounds and buildings. The women used to help on the wards, work as maids on the sick wards, do the washing up or feed the patients. Livesley used to say, '*One for you, one for me*' as she delightedly spooned the mid morning Bovril and bread into an old gentleman. Another would play the piano, another make beautiful carvings out of bits of wood, while others helped in the sewing room, laundry and kitchens. The nurses remember some, especially those who were described as 'simple', with great affection.

As treatment improved in the 50s and 60s, so the railings and high walls were removed.[24] Psychiatry was always the 'Cinderella' service, always at the bottom of the list if ever money was available for improvements. The buildings are at last condemned and are about to be demolished. Patients are resident in the Scarisbrick centre, but mostly are treated as out-patients in the Community.

This, then, was the state of care within the PAI and County Hospital as the Second World War broke out.

Social activities

After a heavy day many nurses still had the energy to raise funds.

Together, they raised money for outings and comforts for the inmates, the sick, and for the wounded soldiers of the first and second world wars.

They produced and provided a Christmas pantomime, Christmas decorations, a Garden Party, a football match, dances and other fun activities, on top of which many of them had to look after husband, home and family.

Ormskirk town also held raffles, bazaars, sports days and other fundraising events for the Institution / Hospital.

Donations from Rushworth and Dreapers (? *Drapers' confectioners in Ormskirk*) raised £300 for the installation of the Hospital Radio. Other businesses in Ormskirk also made contributions.

The main dining room at the hospital and the Working Men's Institute on Moor St were used as venues for dances and entertainments. Garside's (Chemist) and Raymond Winrow gave concerts at Christmas at the Institute. Cowper used the dining room for smaller functions. Trafford ran boxing exhibitions.

They had a lot of fun doing it too! As a consequence, the nurses found they enjoyed a wonderful social life alongside their work. This led to better cooperation when things got difficult on the wards. The nurses developed a sense of owning and belonging to the hospital; their work colleagues became their friends.

The social activities were regularised by the formation of the League of Friends in 1946. The Friends continue to organise fundraising activities. The money is spent on patient welfare. Over the years, they have provided Christmas gifts for Father Christmas himself to deliver, funding for a new scanner and the building of a new Chapel. The list continues to grow.

'Dick Whittington' - produced in the old dining room at Christmas

Fund raising Staff Dance held at the Institution on Moor Street 1940 - 1950

Staff outing to Blackpool 1940 - 1950

Fundraising football match at a Garden Party circa 1950

PREPARATION FOR WAR
Ministry of Health in London and Liverpool

The Emergency Medical Service (EMS) was formed in 1938 to predict and provide medical and hospital services in case of war.

Sir Arthur McNalty, the Chief Medical Officer of Health from Whitehall in London, led the organisation. His chief assistant was Dr John Hobbs (later Sir John Hobbs) who became Principal Medical Officer to the EMS.

Liverpool, as the second largest port in England and with large chemical factories and ship building businesses, was one of the likeliest targets in the country for enemy action. The Ministry appointed Hospital Group Officers into the chief ports, and chief personnel to the cities. They appointed Mr Keith Monsarrat a retired surgeon (aged 73) as their Group Officer in Liverpool. He was given an office in the Liverpool Medical Institution (in what had been the tea room!)

Thankfully, all his letters received from Whitehall, his letters written to Dr Patrick, who held a similar position to himself in Manchester, as well as copies of the letters he wrote to Whitehall have been preserved in the Liverpool Medical Institution.[3]

The correspondence relating to different aspects of the preparation for War is all held in separate folders. One folder dealt with the proposed distribution of casualties from service action, another with schedules for the treatment of the sick of Liverpool. A third estimated the extra bed capacity required in the region for emergency use. Other correspondence in the files dealt with central administration, movement of supplies and items relating to other hospitals in the group. For the following section, I have only acquired information relating to activity in Ormskirk.

Initially, Dr Patrick took the lead from Manchester. However, it soon became apparent that interruption of telephone landlines could lead to serious problems, so from an early stage, each city worked independently.

The Liverpool Group Officer devolved some arrangements to the Medical Officers of Health, Dr WM Frazer, Dr CO Stallybrass and other office staff.

The Liverpool Hospital Staffs Association had been in existence since the end of WW1. This group of senior doctors had joined together to ensure that if War should ever be declared again, they would be organised and prepared. They never, ever, wanted to be as ill-prepared as they had been for WW1 - not just for the logistics, but also for the length of time that the war continued. It was due to their efforts that preparations moved so quickly.

With war imminent there was no place for empire-building. Orders had to be rational and coherent and there needed to be a clear route for dissemination and administration for the many tasks that needed to be completed. This ensured that each wave of hostility and reception of wounded would be dealt with in an orderly way and chaos avoided. Meanwhile the sick of Liverpool had to be accommodated, treated and evacuated to safety as necessary.

To achieve this, the planning chiefs were in continuous consultation with: -

The Emergency sub-committee in Liverpool, the Local Medical War Committees, the British Medical Association, and the Dean of the Faculty of Medicine, Dr Dilling, who commanded the Medical Student Senior Training Corps.

Together they liaised with the Territorial Army Western Command (Chester 3200) to control the movement of personnel. This allowed them direct consultation with the Officer-in-Charge on board each ship or ambulance train as it arrived into the port. They could then work together so that Orders for Disembarkation, De-training and distribution of service (army, navy and air-force) casualties, and POWs could be done seamlessly with dispatch to the most suitable reception facility. The hospital ships and ambulance trains were to be met by an adequate number of stretcher-bearers, ambulances and other vehicles. Suitable personnel were placed in these reception areas to supervise the placing of patients in ambulances and making sure the drivers were aware of their destination. Liaison officers notified the assistant District Medical Superintendent of the receiving hospital with the impending time of arrival and number of casualties.

Negotiations for all these duties were finally settled in the middle of June 1940, by which time, of course, enemy action was well advanced.

There were occasional hiccups; a stationmaster was alerted to the arrival of a train when he had received no instructions from the authorities, so he began a series of strangled squawks that got the whole system upside down!

Each Group Medical Officer was expected to enumerate and provide extra bed capacity for his region. In Liverpool, this amounted to an extra 1850 beds.

He was also required to identify peripheral hospitals and public assistance institutions, where there was sufficient space to build extra accommodation (beds) within hutments. These would then cater for the medical needs of the region should Liverpool be put out of action and provide extra capacity for military purposes.

The peripheral hospitals involved were Whiston, Broadgreen, St Helens (Peasley Cross), Alder Hey, Ormskirk PAI, Southport and Wrightington.

There had already been a survey of the Lancashire hospitals set up by Lord Nuffield's Provincial Hospital Trust in the early 1930s. This was done as a prelude for legislation to provide some uniformity of services throughout the country. This brief summary is all I could find specifically relating to the General Hospital in Ormskirk.

"Small general hospital of approximately 45 beds. No resident medical officer, theatre and wards poor and nurses accommodation unattractive. Some vacant land."

In fact this hospital had no maternity services, no mental health facility and could not perform any major surgery unless a surgeon was brought in from Liverpool.[10i]

The PAI in Ormskirk by contrast had considerable land. It had a small psychiatric service and a tiny maternity unit for the Institution residents.

It was decided to build six new hutted wards and an operating theatre suite there, thus creating a complete Ormskirk County Hospital. The General Hospital later known as 'The Brandreth' continued as before to provide medical services for the town.

The huts to be built via the Ministry of Works were of differing grades, A, B and C. A and B huts were to be placed on existing hospital or PAI sites as temporary extra accommodation. The C grade huts were more substantial and could be used as the basis for a new hospital at the end of the war.

The Local Authority was expected to pay a rental of 4% of the cost of construction of C grade huts over a period of 25 years. The Local Authority was also expected to take on the responsibility of ownership including repair and maintenance .[21]

'Our' huts were said to be temporary, i.e. A or B grade, but in fact were in use for over 40 years!

This new accommodation was to be used for sick evacuees from other parts of the country, evacuated air-raid casualties of Liverpool and evacuated civilian patients. It was also to accommodate sick Liverpool residents from central hospitals, fit to travel, but unfit for discharge. The huts were also to accommodate some service (army, navy and air force) personnel including overseas Allies and POWs.

The Northern Hospital, St Paul's Eye Hospital, Walton and Aintree Hospitals would send their overflow to Ormskirk, Wrightington and Southport. The Royal Infirmary, Royal Southern Hospital, Mill Road Hospital and Bootle Hospital would send their overflow to St Helens, Whiston and Alder Hey.

However, Whiston's hutted accommodation was delayed and only become available from April 1941, so the other hospitals had to share the load between them.

Walton Hospital offered to send, if necessary, surgical equipment, a maximum of two assistant resident surgical officers, a theatre sister and four to five theatre assistants to Ormskirk.

Similar arrangements were made to other peripheral units by the other Liverpool hospitals.

Each Medical Superintendent of the various hospitals in the Region was to keep an Admission and Discharge Book. He was to be held responsible for the records of each patient as laid down in the regulations.

The Admission and Discharge book for Ormskirk has not been traced nor have the records, and so I have had to use the figures from the Master and Matrons' Report to get some idea of the numbers of sick and injured involved.

It is at this time too that hospitals began to specialise in certain types of injuries. Sefton took renal problems, Broadgreen took chests, Walton took neurological, and Whiston took the burns.

The preparations were all too soon put to the test.

In 1940 alone 14 hospital ships disembarked in Liverpool.

The last was on August 20th 1945.

Bomb damage to hospital windows caused serious interference with work. On six occasions, hospitals in Liverpool had to be completely evacuated and were out of commission for a week or two because the theatres and wards could not be lit at night.

The first large consignment of patients to Ormskirk was brought from London Hospitals damaged by enemy action.

The first substantial service casualties were received from the Norwegian Campaign in June 1940.

Letter to KW Monsarrat FRCS from Hobbs of the Ministry of Health, Whitechapel; '*I am concerned that these cases from Norway should go to a suitably staffed hospital capable of dealing with frostbite. I am anxious that you (Mr Monserrat) will curb the enthusiasm of the younger surgeons who have little or no experience of managing such cases (of frostbite) and are unaware of the powers of recovery in the terminal parts of limbs. They might thus avoid unnecessary amputations.*' This particular contingent of frostbitten men were disembarked pick-a-back to avoid further damage to their feet by Hospital Ship *Atlantis* in Liverpool at the end of May 1940, but did not go to Ormskirk.[7]

12th June 1940

The Hospital Ship Atlantis	Berthed at 9am
Full complement of 435 patients	Disembarked at 10am
	194 patients to Ormskirk
101 walking injured	
93 stretcher cases	
2 with diphtheria	Dispatched to Fazakerley
1 with cerebrospinal malaria	infectious diseases unit
3 Specials + 1 other ranked	Royal infirmary
Ormskirk County took 115 walking cases,	69 Allied, 46 British
	15 other stretcher cases, 3 British
	12 Allied
	49 German POW
	30 other ranks

This large contingent was sent to Ormskirk County Hospital because of the want of further accommodation at Davyhulme Military Hospital. (Presumably the remaining patients were admitted to Davyhulme)

2nd November 1940   Evacuees (from London) detrained at Aintree:-

30 Male stretcher cases
68 Female stretcher cases
57 Male sitting injured
117 Female sitting injured
Total 272

Female walking injured sent to Wrightington	35	1 bus and 2 cars
Female walking injured sent to Ormskirk	82	3 buses
Male walking injured sent to Ormskirk	39	1 bus and 3 cars
Female stretcher cases sent to Ormskirk	21	2 large ambulances Hand
luggage went with the patients.		1 small ambulance

Van luggage was distributed on November 3rd by 2 vans supplied by the Chief Ambulance Officer

16th February 1945	24 lying cases were sent to Ormskirk
11th May 1945	84 walking cases were sent to Ormskirk
29th June 1945	4 Polish sent to Ormskirk

It is not clear in these later lists, which Ormskirk Hospital (County or Military) was to be used. However, the nurses' stories and the Master and Matron's report from the PAI (EMS) describe reception of a large contingent from Norway in June 1940, and the evacuees were certainly sent to the EMS hospital, but the destination of those sent in 1945 is less clear. Certainly EMS continued to receive Convoys from overseas until the end of the war, and also convalescents until 1946.

Details of the sick and injured received into the County are recorded in the section provided by the nurses in a later part of this story, mostly substantiated by the Master and Matron's report.[5]

Preparations for War in Ormskirk

Directions from the Ministry in London via Liverpool gave the **Local Authorities** their own powers to respond to any local emergencies as a result of war. All senior officials in the town (including the Medical Officer) took part in the planning for every eventuality and formed a close network of communications between all departments. The Master of the Institution had to plan for a sudden surge of admissions or for complete evacuation at short notice on orders from any department of the Authority.[21] Arrangements were made for local householders to accept evacuated adults or children from other areas, so that when people arrived, there would be places ready for them. These arrangements would apply for local emergencies too, as an air base was situated in Burscough and there were lookout posts within the Authority boundaries where personnel could be affected in an attack.

Discussions were held about how to cope with unofficial evacuees, whether they were eligible for emergency financial relief etc. It was decided that clothing could be provided but not rent, unless no other source of rent could be found.

The mothers' clinic became the place for the sale and provision of National Dried Milk powder, concentrated orange juice and vitamins to augment the poor diet of wartime British mothers and babies.

Minster Lodge on Ruff Lane was requisitioned to house sick evacuated children.

Later in the War, Scarisbrick Hall was used as a convalescent centre to relieve pressure on the County Hospital.

Other services were arranged by the **Urban District Army Social Welfare Committee** as the war progressed and the needs were determined.[6]

For example, a library book service with a chance to talk to the library worker was arranged for both the County and Military Hospitals.

Lady visitors were recruited to visit the men in the hospitals many of whom were far from home.

They arranged hospitality for friends and family visiting men in the military hospitals; a car from Liverpool or Whiston and one night free accommodation if necessary. This was often very difficult to organise.

Adoption of isolated Anti-aircraft posts by local families for off-duty periods were rather easier to arrange, but the request that the WRVS collect and mend socks was not entertained at all!

Permission was granted for dances to be held in the town, partly as a fund-raising exercise but also to keep young people off the streets.

The General Hospital in Hants Lane continued to look after the sick of Ormskirk as before. Many staff members were conscripted into war service, leaving older and less able staff to carry on as best they could. The previous arrangements for Maternity care at the Christiana Hartley Unit in Southport, and for surgical care in Liverpool, ceased except for the most complicated cases. Some of these activities were then transferred to 'the County' where new facilities existed.

General Practitioners were responsible for extra Public Health Duties; they had to visit the air raid shelters regularly, checking for infectious diseases and infestation. Fleas and scabies were endemic! They were also responsible for treating possible civilian casualties of Burscough, Scarisbrick and Aughton. Many GPs, however, were called up for active service, leaving older doctors to cope with an increasingly heavy workload.

Alongside these War preparations led by the Local Authority, **the Military** were also making their own preparations for recruiting, training, and equipping men and women for War. They took over many large houses and institutions for this purpose. Some of these houses were to be used as military hospitals or POW camps.

The Windmill at Bickerstaffe held Italians who were supervised and worked in the local farms. They wore a yellow disc on the back of their clothing.

Wimbrick House and Asmall Hall were both requisitioned for housing POWs, as both these houses were surrounded by a wall and easy to police.[23]

In 1939 at short notice, the Territorial Army (TA) requisitioned Edge Hill College as their Hospital.

Extra accommodation was built in hutted wards, as in the EMS hospital.

These were more substantial though, and built of brick. The huts brought their bed capacity to 600. The huts were only finished after the EMS ones, so that early military sick or casualties were admitted to the EMS Hospital.

I could find no records to study about the work of Edge Hill. I contacted the TA in Liverpool without any papers being found.

I contacted the Military Museum in Aldershot at the Keogh Barracks, but again gained no information. Nor was there anything to be found in the Liverpool Record Office. Apart from a single list of illnesses treated (January to June 1944) found in the National Archives, nothing more was discovered about the war time activity in Ormskirk Military Hospital.[8]

The following information is an amalgamation of what I have been told.

There was a fully operational theatre and X-ray facility. The hospital was staffed with military medical and nursing personnel. The matron was a member of the Queen Alexandra's Royal Army Nursing Corps (QA). There were some ancillary staff recruited from the local community.

Many of their patients were orthopaedic cases and the wheelchairs and slings of the men in their 'blues' coming down St Helens Road are well remembered.

However, the one report, mentioned above, suggests that there were a considerable number of cases of amoebic dysentery and tuberculosis.

There was some exchange of personnel at times of crisis. Nursing staff from the Military Hospital came to help the County during the Liverpool Blitz, and the County Hospital psychiatric unit was used to treat some of the military shell-shocked patients. The County Hospital was also used to conduct post-mortem examinations for certain military cases.

The Military Hospital at Edge Hill was referred to as 'the 29th' or 'the 102nd', suggesting that it was used by different units at different times during the war. I have been unable to establish what these numbers signify. The Military Hospital closed on 21st June 1944 and the remaining patients were sent to the military hospital in Chester, or for convalesance. The buildings were then known as the Polish Hospital because of the number of allies remaining there. The Ormskirk Urban District Army Social Welfare Committee reported that *in August 1945, Nº. 4 Polish General Hospital (at Edge Hill) had transferred to Whitchurch'.

After the war the building reverted to a Teacher Training College.

From Grace Hardisty, who volunteered for FANY (First Aid Nursing Yeomanry) as an ambulance driver. She worked from Preston Headquarters and was seconded to Squire's Gate Training Camp for the Pioneer Corps in Blackpool. She drove sick conscripts from the unit to the Military Hospital (Edge Hill).

One night, by mistake at the beginning of the war, she delivered her ambulance to the EMS, only to get a flea in her ear for delivering to the wrong hospital! She remembers with great pleasure 'her' vehicle. It was a left hand drive, wonderfully sprung Chevrolet donated by the Canadians. The tiny front lights just about lit the kerb edge as she drove in the black-out.

Later on, she was involved with driving ambulances full of injured men (capacity 4 stretchers) from the Liverpool docks and evacuees to other hospitals, though not to Ormskirk.

All this preparation in Ormskirk meant that once hostilities commenced there was a clear and orderly sequence of actions to be taken for any emergency. It was all very well on paper but in reality there was some initial chaos!

WARTIME AT THE COUNTY

The Master and Matron's Report Book gives an insight into the preparations and changes brought to the sick wards of the Institution as they were developed into a full hospital catering for all the needs of a General Hospital in wartime.

In May 1939, Senior Planning officers from the EMS in Liverpool visited the Institution

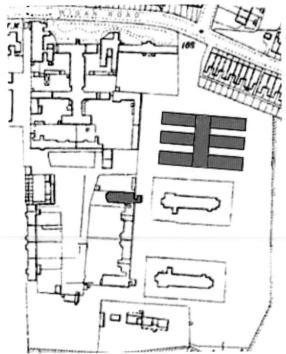

to discuss the plans to build six single-storey wooden huts as wards and create a new theatre suite within the existing maternity unit.

Each hut would hold forty-two beds. There would be no side rooms or day rooms, just two bathrooms, with toilets, bath and wash hand basin, a sister's office, a sluice and a tiny kitchen. The floors were of black asphalt and there were three coke stoves down the length of each ward for heating.

The workhouse maternity unit was upgraded. The whole of the lower ground floor of the women's building was converted into two operating theatres with changing rooms, ante-room and scrub area.

Maternity was then moved to the two upper floors of the same building but access to the theatre was external only. The women who had been on these floors were moved to other areas in the institution.

Staff from Walton Hospital also visited to discuss the arrangements for emergency transfer of patients from Walton to Ormskirk if war conditions made it necessary.

They also discussed and agreed transfer of surgical equipment and staff to service the new operating theatres.

By August 1939, sandbags and tea chests of soil were placed around various buildings as an Air Raid Precaution (ARP). Gas masks were issued to everyone, and an ARP station was established within cellars under the Master's house. This entailed the removal of 100 years of accumulated 'stores' from the cellars!

Blackout material and blinds were bought, extra beds purchased and plans were made for dealing with a possible air raid attack.

The kitchen was inspected with a view to extending the facilities necessary for the extra 250 patients expected on the new wards.

The farm was more intensively cultivated to provide vegetables for the hospital, and the land between the new wards was planted with potatoes. There were pigs too, kept in the area by the Works Department.

Staff levels had to be increased.

By early 1940, due to lack of casuals or suitable inmates, two additional gardeners had to be employed.

Dr HC Haslam Fox was appointed Medical Superintendent. For many years he had been the Public Vaccinator and Visiting Medical Officer to the Institution as well as running a very successful General Practice in Ormskirk and Skelmersdale. Dr JD Craig and Dr WP O'Regan (GPs already working in the town of Ormskirk), were appointed to assist Dr Fox. They helped look after the workhouse areas and the new hospital. Dr Fox occasionally helped to check the black-out and security of the huts, the residents did the rest.

A Radiologist, Dr R Steele and Pathologist, Dr R Y Dawbarn were employed. Other staff were seconded from Walton Hospital.

Dr Styles, Dr Pugh, Dr Ansell, Dr Porterfield and Dr Cameron all spent time at Ormskirk as residents. A team of visiting Specialists also attended.

Surgeons Mr Heany, Mr Kelly and Mr Kirk-Wilson came from Liverpool aided by registrar Mr Moroney who later wrote a nurses training textbook.

Mr Walsh was appointed consultant for Gynaecology and Obstetrics and Dr Murray Bligh and Dr Littler for General Medicine. There was also a Mr Baleshaew (the spelling of this name is uncertain) - a surgeon from Poland. This influx of staff created a need for more staff accommodation, so the female casual (tramp) ward was closed in June 1940, and was converted for use by 3 resident medical staff, a medical Registrar and Military Staff.

Doris Foster *Sybil Barnes née Critchley*

Bet Farrington in Civil Nursing Reserve Uniforms

EMS ward (hut) during the blackout 1940

The boundary wall alongside Ruff Lane was broached to allow access by a disabled member of the medical staff.

Miss Newsham, a QA was appointed Matron.

Miss Morris was in charge of the Theatres and Sister Draper was the first Theatre Sister. More nurses were needed to staff the new hutted wards. More than 80 Civilian Nursing Reserves were recruited and trained. Accommodation had to be found for these new nurses outside the hospital.

At the beginning of the war, there was no shortage of volunteers to the nursing service. These Nursing Auxiliaries (Naggie Annies, Naughty Annies) received a basic four-week training at Preston.

Enrolled Nurses were sent to Walton for surgical training. Their course lasted only six weeks.

There was no national nurse training system in place at this time. Senior staff nurses and Sisters trained their juniors. They were often very strict but the nurses are united in their praise of the system that gave them a good grounding in all aspects of nursing care. However, there was definitely, as Pat Starkey in her book of 'Nursing Memories' reports, '*a hierarchical subversiveness in the system as opposed to professionalism. Nurses' uniform reflected the old ideas of servants' wear, and the patients expected the nurses to 'fetch and carry' for them. Girls entering nursing from the middle and upper classes went into the more prestigious teaching and large private hospitals. Secondary schoolgirls were more likely to be accepted into the municipal (ex-workhouse) hospitals. On marriage, nurses were expected to resign their positions. However the war changed all that and more married nurses were employed*'.[16]

Grudgingly, it was acknowledged that these married women, because of their life experience made very good, if not better, nurses.

Some women with ARP training also joined.

Though many joined, many more left because of poor working conditions, and because of the fleas!

The turnover was so high that there were not enough volunteers and more women had to be called up for service. Hairdressers and confectioners, domestic staff and nursemaids were all conscripted.

NAs wore a Saxe blue uniform with a red NA stitched on the front. They wore white caps. These items were laundered at the hospital or at Whitley's in Southport.

Those nurses who already had some experience wore a white uniform and caps. Outside Uniform consisted of an air force blue gabardine coat and navy felt hat with CNR (Civil Nursing Reserve) embroidered on it.

Other changes brought to the Institution had to do with the need for increased security. The Lodge Porter was instructed in extra security procedures. Fixed bayonets were mounted on the hospital gates, which by 1940 had been made of solid wood.

Next came the testing period of Civil Exercises.

An 'Evacuation of Hospital' telegram was received. Within three hours, fifty residents had been sent by ambulance and WVS cars to alternative accommodation. On the next day another 26 were discharged.

This was confirmed by a minute from Fleetwood Road Hospital in Blackpool, which stated that, *some aged women were transferred from Ormskirk PAI. These cases were selected by the MOH. All the bedfast cases are incontinent.' This hospital has 62 beds.*[19] (As this hospital has only 27 beds now, did this transfer cause serious overcrowding?)

I was told by a reliable source of a seriously ill patient in another hospital who was transferred in a specially adapted double-decker bus to another 'safer' hospital on a similar exercise. The condition of those to be moved was not considered, and the move in this case was seriously detrimental. The beds in the receiving hospital were so close together that it was almost impossible to walk between them.

Major Worthington and Captain Lowe undertook military administrative duties for the huts. They took charge of the soldiers' uniform on admission, dealt with disciplinary matters and communicated with relatives.

Meanwhile, of course, the work of the institution continued and expanded as the years passed. In the whole of 1940, 357 persons were admitted into the residential part of the Institution; there were 130 sick admissions and 193 casuals. In addition, the hospital accepted more and more local residents for medical or surgical care.

Separate records were kept for the new EMS admissions.

All was not gloom, however, and at times something happened to make everyone brighter. For example, in the middle of the early records on 13 January 1940 was a delighted, *'Mrs Banks had living triplets'.*[5]

The admission rate varied enormously. At times, there were large convoys of injured soldiers, then there would be injured civilians from the bombing raids, and then it would be quieter again.

These numbers of admissions per month were recorded, and varied from 522 for the Liverpool May Blitz of 1941 to 52 in July 1943. Discharge levels were equally variable. The arrival of evacuees from the London Blitz early in 1940 came before the preparations or hutments were complete.

Many of the new admissions from the London Blitz were heaving with lice by the time they reached Ormskirk. A number of the newly trained NAs couldn't cope and left! They had expected that they would be nursing the grateful sick and injured, and found some of the patients foul-mouthed, far from grateful, and desperate to go home.

The Female hospital Wards Top and Bottom wings were taken over for these Emergency admissions.

The Male hospital wards became the new wards for County and Southport cases. The Bottom Wing remained as a Male Institution hospital of 28 beds.

You can sense the feeling of panic in the following report in the Master's book.

'The main kitchen is being enlarged. Getting hot meals to the top wards is a problem as the nurses have to walk the food up, two plates at a time from the ground floor.
Laundry for the EMS is being carried to an outside laundry.
There is no telephone connection.'

The new wards finally opened in June 1940.

Wounded soldiers soon followed the evacuees.

According to the minutes of the Public Assistance Board the first convoy arrived on the 12th of June 1940 and consisted of 130 allied soldiers. The nurses said these men came from Narvik, and that all the men were Polish. The common language was French. Lady Scarisbrick valiantly came over to help translate and some of the NAs had enough French to help with translation. (This tallies with the report from the Hospital Ship *Atlantis* [7])

Later there were men from Dunkirk. This convoy also had some French soldiers who later joined the British army.

Other men travelled by train from other parts of the country to Aintree where they were placed in Army Ambulances for transfer to the receiving hospital. Most transfers were done at night.

A ward was cleared for each convoy, to control cross infection and also to keep the men together as a unit.

Of the six huts, at one time, one was full of TB cases and another was allocated to Officers.

Staff always had to be careful as more than one injured man was from the nefarious 5th Column of German Spies.

Most of the injured had relatively minor injuries such as gunshot wounds.

Men were admitted in their 'Blues' and red tie. Each man was given a field card, which had to be filled in and posted to his next of kin. This card confirmed arrival in the UK as many had been previously listed as '*missing presumed dead.*'

On admission, after the initial administrative business was over, each man was settled in his own bed with a curtain-fronted locker for personal items and a chair. Wheeled screens were used for privacy during bathing, bedpan use and when dressings were done. Extra beds might be put up in the middle of the ward if required.

As soon as possible, the injured man was taken to theatre to have his dressings taken down. His wounds would be assessed and plans made for further treatment.

For this to be accomplished, he was placed on a trolley and wheeled across to theatre. The theatre was across the access road and about a hundred yards away in a separate building. There were no milk floats (open ambulances run by batteries) in those days, just an umbrella if it rained or snowed!

In 1948, a patient Pat Ramsay recalled, 'We had an austere experience of hospital life, silent ward rounds, no choice of menu, little entertainment from a wireless and no library, but the physical nursing care each patient received was exceptional - and necessary at a time when there weren't today's drugs. . . A wonderfully cheery Lizzie came in very early every morning to rake out and riddle the ashes and coax the fire into new life. The fire was tended several times a day and we were kept warm, but the dust and fumes came and went depending on the wind direction. The beds were hard and lumpy and the blankets heavy and not very warm. And there was that awful rubber sheet underneath . . . Mobile screens gave little privacy, and the bedpans were either too hot or freezing . . . and the daily question, 'Have you been?'. . . .The corridor joining the wards had a roof but no sides so the draught really swept into the bathrooms and wards. . . .The journey to X-ray or theatre was quite an experience. You travelled on a rather hard trolley. Over you was placed a canvas-covered frame with a piece of Perspex let into the top to give a little light. The whole thing was horribly suggestive of a bottomless coffin – but it kept the rain out and we survived!'

Anaesthetic agents were not easy to obtain as most of those produced were sent out to the War Zones. Because of this, much of the surgery was done using Evapan, a rectal anaesthetic or spinal block used according to body weight.

Injuries were initially treated in the dressing stations out in the field. Wounds were cleaned there and covered with Vaseline gauze; Plaster of Paris was then applied to immobilise the area as much as possible.

After several days of travelling, it is not surprising that many wounds had become badly infected; even gangrenous if the plaster was too tight, and often full of maggots. The wounds full of maggots were noted to be the cleanest and these were the ones which healed the best. From this experience has come the modern use of maggots in the treatment of persistent ulcers.

Post-operatively the nurses would wheel their patients back to the ward, carrying any drip bottle on high!

Those patients who were bomb-happy (shell-shocked) would be taken across to the Pavilions (psychiatric Unit) for treatment. These men were expected to help on the wards, collecting dishes, washing up etc. as part of their therapy. Charge Nurse, Mr Diggle, attended them.

Towards the end of 1940, it was recorded that only three huts were being used by the military in the EMS, but that there were nearly 400 beds in use at the Military Hospital. The balance was soon redressed by the admission of 141 sick civilians from London, quickly followed by another 66 Military patients.

The difficulties were compounded by the fact that the ambulances kept breaking down and it was necessary to liaise with the 29th Military Hospital for transport.

Combined with this large influx of patients, and difficulty with transport, the Master's report states that, 'on the 8th November 1940 at 9.30 pm a High Explosive Bomb fell in the grounds of the Institution, 15ft from the main entrance, and 10ft from the main road. There is a 6ft x 12ft crater. No casualties were reported and only slight damage was done. Paving stones were found on the roof of the Lodge'.

Only 3 bombs landed in Ormskirk. This one at the hospital, one at Edge Hill, and a third near Hattersleys Brass Foundry on Burscough Road.

Apart from this there was little enemy action over Ormskirk, though the Children's ward veranda rattled with ack-ack vibrations from time to time.

Veranda of the Children's ward showing the outdoor beds

Soldier patients by the open corridor between the huts

There was another brief lull in military activity in April 1941, when only 4 soldiers were left, but this was more than compensated for by the admission of 91 air raid casualties and transferred sick from Walton hospital.

May 1941 saw the Liverpool Blitz.

During this month there were an incredible number of patients seen. Luckily many were only in the hospital briefly, but the records show,

Total Admissions 522   Discharged 529

Relatives walked out from Liverpool to Ormskirk looking for lost family members. They slept in Churches, Institutes and shelters on their way. It was a strange sight to see so many dazed folk camping with their gas masks. Many had lost everyone and everything.

Matron and staff from the 29th Military Hospital helped the EMS cope with this influx of air raid casualties.

Scarisbrick Hall set up a convalescent facility for air raid casualties and for some children. Keith Monsarrat, CMO of Liverpool and in charge of the EMS services, came out of his dark windowless office in the Liverpool Medical Institution to help organise the refugees from the Blitz. Every pair of hands available was needed and appreciated!

He would occasionally come out to Ormskirk at the weekend, glad to be offered some fresh food from the hospital farm, and to be with colleagues he had worked with in the Cottage Hospital before his retirement.

As a result of this very busy period, a blood transfusion service was established in the Male House. This meant that in June 1941, forty male inmates had to be transferred to another institution to allow use of their ward by the hospital.

What the men thought of this sudden transfer is not recorded.

As part of the Nuffield Hospital Survey of Lancashire Hospitals, Rock Carling and Mr Monsarrat visited in September 1942. Their report was only published in 1945.[10ii]

Civil Exercises continued. In December 1942, 380 cases were admitted – twice in 24 hours. Where they put the 'casualties' is not recorded!

Unsurprisingly the report states, *'The Male wards are overcrowded.'*

On top of this the records show 189 EMS admissions of which 140 were discharged within the month.

Permission was granted for bodies from the Military Hospital to be received at the County for post-mortem examination. Only certain named deceased were brought to the County, and always with special permission being granted. All that I saw in the records were either Polish or German.

By June 1943, things were getting fraught once more. The work was unrelenting and heavy. There were long lists of temporary staff and huge staff shortages.

This led to the following comment in the report book, *'There is extra staff accommodation all over the place . This is most inconvenient with files and books being carried from one end of the institution to the other.'*

New military cases continued to be admitted alongside the civilian sick of Ormskirk and overflow from Walton Hospital. Stories that there were no more military patients after the initial admissions are untrue as there are records of military admissions right through the war period to August 1945, and some undated admissions after the liberation.

86 were admitted in October 1943, and another 37 came for their meals only. Presumably these extra meals were for men convalescent and resident in the area.

Very clear in the minds of some nurses, over 50 years later, was the admission in May/June 44 of a convoy of 56 Military patients from North Africa. All were spinal injuries, lying in plaster cases.

These men had been made to jump out of their vehicles and lie flat on the desert sand. They were then shot through the spine. Once stabilised, some of the men were transferred via London to Stoke Mandeville Hospital. Others eventually were returned to specialist hospitals nearer their own homes. Some even travelled with a nurse escort to the Scottish highlands. This was a great treat for the escorting nurse, especially if she had relatives there.

That same month of June 1944, another 40 men were admitted from France, 27 from Italy, and then another 40 from Italy.

In August 1944, there were yet more Military admissions from several different sources. Many of these were at the convalescent stage of recovery, but not yet fit for discharge.

Farewell Dinner before the transfer of the last military patients 1945

From the left; Mrs Blundell Chair of Guardians, Dr Haslam Fox,
Matron Boyle, Miss Morris, Home Sister O'Hara and Mr Beck Superintendent

France	80	Algiers (Merchant Navy)	10
Southport	20 walking	Northern Hospital (Overseas)	6
Manchester Royal	7	France via Alder Hey	16
Liverpool Royal	6	Italy	24

In October 1944, 50 stretcher cases came from Italy and another 128 civilians were accepted.

In November 1944, 38 stretcher cases came from France

In May 1945, convoys carrying 64 stretcher cases from Italy arrived, with 21 German POWs and another 62 wounded men.

German and Japanese POWs were received and even a few men liberated from Belsen, suffering from severe malnutrition arrived with their nurse escorts.

As with the spinal injury cases from 1944, some patients were transferred to hospitals nearer their own home; with or without a nurse escort. A military ambulance would carry them as far as Lime St Station. The train would then take them the next stage of the journey and an ambulance would meet them at the other end. At times, the journey was interrupted by enemy action, but mostly passed without incident.

May/June 45   EMS admissions 277, discharges 303

October   45   A convoy of 41 Military were admitted from Burma

December 45   EMS Admissions 101, discharged 185 + convoys of Military 63 were admitted.

In February 1946 a convoy of 94 EMS cases were received from Europe followed by another 50.

Eventually in May 1946 all the remaining military patients were transferred to Southport EMS.

As the EMS beds emptied of military patients, so they were filled with chronic sick patients from the temporary military hospitals such as Edge Hill. This explains a note in the Master's report that, 'It is understood that 60 chronic sick EMS patients will be received from Kirkham'. Residents of the Ormskirk Institution who had been boarded out for the duration were also returned.

A request for the return of X-ray equipment to Walton Hospital in September 1946 was refused and as no further comment was made, I must assume the items were retained by the County Hospital.

This great list of hospital activity shows how vital was the contribution made by Ormskirk to the injured of the Second World War.

Social Care

In addition to all the skilled nursing and medical care given to the sick and injured, great efforts were made to provide entertainment and visitors for the patients, most of whom were a long way from home. Travelling for their family was difficult and at times dangerous.

The British Legion arranged for their members to visit the men in hospital. They also hired wireless sets for the hospital.

ENSA (Entertainments National Service Association) via Liverpool provided some entertainment and produced concerts for small groups of men.

The wards were often visited officially, by Lady Redding of the WRVS, Miss Jones, Matron of Liverpool Royal Infirmary,[17] who had a responsibility for nurses' welfare, and unofficially by Lady Scarisbrick.

Miss Griffiths, one of the senior nurses, would make sure she was off duty whenever Miss Jones arrived. NO WAY would Miss Griffiths wear her cap to cover all her hair! She was an excellent nurse though and was awarded the Military Medal for her war work. I remember well how in the sixties she was prepared to roll up her sleeves and help when the wards were understaffed at night. She was a great inspiration to her juniors.

Food was never a big problem for Ormskirk. The institution farm was very productive and there was never any shortage of vegetables and potatoes.

The people of Skelmersdale and Kirkby would visit each month on a rota bringing tea for the wards. At this time of course the new towns had not been built, and both towns were very small rural communities. The nurses appreciated the leftovers!

One patient, Edna, was thought to have coeliac disease so a call went out over the wireless for bananas, and they arrived by the crate load!

As the clinical condition of the men improved, they were allowed more freedom.

In June 1944, one of the hutted wards was made into a recreation room. It was divided into three sections, a canteen, a quiet room with a library, and a billiard room. Col Orowski was in charge. He organised dominoes and whist drives. Occasionally dances were arranged and quizzes held.

Nurses in their off-duty time would wheel patients out into Ormskirk and even as far as the Ryburn Tea Rooms on the way to Southport. Some nurses took patients to their own homes for a break.

Convalescent soldiers and staff between the huts and Wigan Road houses

Wedding Party at St. Anne's, centre: Dr Styles and Night Sister Alcock 1945

Soldiers were allowed one late pass a week up to 8pm. This rule was regularly and frequently broken. They were smuggled out in the back of nurses' cars, lying on the back seat and sat on by nurses. It was not uncommon to see crutches appear over the wall and then bodies sneak into the wards through the French windows. Other patients kept guard so that when the night round was done by torch light in the black-out, a man after being checked on one side of the ward would creep out and fill a bed on the other side!

If caught, the soldier would be CB (confined to barracks) for a week!

Though Ormskirk was known to be pretty dead in the evenings, there was a nightclub on Burscough St, known as the Monkey Nest. Americans from the aerodrome in Burscough went there and were a great attraction to some of the local girls who wanted to let their hair down after a heavy working day. Local lads would scorn *those* girls!

Recently, men who had been in hospital during the war revisited Ormskirk. They publicly expressed their appreciation of all the hard work that had gone into their care.

POST WAR DEVELOPMENT OF THE HOSPITAL

In 1946, the Liverpool Regional Hospital Board became the Liverpool Regional Health Authority and by 1948, the Ormskirk County Hospital was transferred to the National Health Service (NHS).[22] In 1948, Miss Jones, Matron of the Royal Infirmary, visited in her capacity as Senior Sister for the Liverpool Regional Hospital Board. She recorded 400 occupied beds of which 41 were for children.[9]

With the advent of the NHS, residential institutional care for the destitute was no longer required. However, most of the inmates remaining in the institution were considered too institutionalised, too elderly or too sick to be returned into the community. They were gradually dispersed for long term care to Greaves Hall or Sefton House (men) and the Maghull Homes (women). Chronic young disabled patients were transferred to a specialist centre, such as a Leonard Cheshire Home. The final distribution of Institution residents was completed in 1960. It was in this year, too, that the railings around the psychiatric block were finally removed.[24]

In 1948, the EMS huts which had been only partly used since the end of the war became part of the new Ormskirk and District General Hospital (ODGH). It was and still is referred to as 'the County'!

From 1960 to 1980, a Nurse Training School was established for training Assistant Nurses and for Part II of the midwife's course.

Nurses training for the Register of General Nursing also had to complete a midwifery component of six weeks working on the maternity unit. The Nurse Training and Midwifery Schools were phased out as the training curriculum developed. General Nurse and Maternity nurse training are now degree courses prior to working on the wards.

Within a year of the inception of the NHS, the cost of food was no longer taken out of nurses' wages. This was a relief as many nurses didn't eat hospital food anyway. The nursing day staff were given an extra half-day off in three weeks, and were expected to clean their own rooms in this time! Night duty changed to a rota of five nights on and two off.

By 1952, the wages were approximately £19 per month.

In 1952, the Bed capacity of ODGH was 406, with 126 in the Psychiatric department. Elizabeth and Philip wards were built for surgical cases in 1953 and named to commemorate the Coronation of Queen Elizabeth II.

Post War EMS Ward (hut)

Dr. Fox retained his interest in the Maternity and Psychiatric wards. He only retired when his eyesight began to fail him. I assisted him with his last Caesarean Section in 1963. His work on the psychiatric and maternity units was continued by General Practitioners for some years until specialist juniors were appointed to the wards.

Lifts were installed to the maternity and geriatric wards in the mid 1960s and at last the nurses, porters and ambulance staff no longer had to carry patients, infants, or food up and down the stairs. New toilet blocks were constructed for these wards to provide showers, more baths and toilets.

Despite the arrival in 1964 of New Town Skelmersdale with its young population, the maternity unit had only four labour rooms, one of which still had the 'en suite' lavatory. This says something for the local birth rate. The labour suite was finally condemned in the 1970s, and a new suite of delivery rooms were constructed within the original area, and the lying-in wards were modernised to provide more privacy

Further modernisation of the wards was effected throughout the hospital,

With the advent of more sophisticated treatments inpatient care has been drastically curtailed. Many conditions can now be treated at home and many surgical procedures are performed as day-cases. On the maternity unit, hospital stays are reduced from a minimum of delivery only with discharge shortly afterwards, to five days for a Caesarean section.

The new hospital has far fewer beds than the original.

Ormskirk remained part of the Liverpool Regional Health Authority until boundary changes and other political changes of 1974 linked us with Manchester. Despite these 'official' links, many of the older doctors and those who trained in Liverpool still preferred to send their patients to Liverpool.

As always, transport is still the problem of getting to Manchester.

In 1980, Bickerstaffe House and the Scarisbrick centre were built and at last the facilities for treating Mental Health conditions began to be addressed.

The problems of a split site and of maintaining the old buildings was ever increasing, so that when the first phase of a new hospital was shelved again in 1988 there was a national outcry. This focused particularly on the antiquated transport of patients to theatre along the open road.

Domestic and canteen services were then privatised. This called for a number of redundancies and the beginnings of a feeling of unrest. So it was with relief that in 1989, phase 1 of the new hospital was begun.

In 2003, creation of the NHS Trusts and reduction of resident doctors' hours in the training grades united the hospitals of Ormskirk and Southport. Rationalisation of the services provided by the two hospitals resulted in the acute medical and surgical facilities with Intensive and Coronary care being kept at Southport, and Maternity and Child Health Services in Ormskirk.

Now, once again, the problem is that of transport from the outlying districts of West Lancashire to these Hospitals and even from Ormskirk to Southport along the very busy A570.

The Post Graduate Medical Centre and Nurse Training Development Centre are being used in conjunction with Edge Hill University for the degree course of Nurse Training and Health Studies. They house a library and lecture facilities.

The Post Graduate Medical Centre hosts one of few national societies for retired medical personnel, appropriately named 'The Brandreth Club'.

Post War changes in other hospitals and Sanatoria in Ormskirk

The General Hospital was renamed the Cottage Hospital. Gradually the acute work done there was transferred to ODGH. This left some geriatric care, out-patient day-care, a diabetic clinic and day-case surgery. These functions too were gradually transferred to ODGH, leaving only a few beds for chronic geriatric care and a day care centre for the elderly. At this point The Cottage Hospital was renamed 'The Brandreth' after an eminent Ormskirk physician of the 18th century. The elderly residents were transferred to care homes in the Community and a new day care facility was built on Derby Street. The Brandreth then closed.

The buildings and land, formerly owned by Lord Derby, were sold to the Ormskirk and Skelmersdale College of Further Education.

Ormskirk, Lathom and Burscough District Council ran **Green Lane Hospital**. This was a hospital for Children, for chronic infection such as tuberculosis and acute infections such as scarlet fever, diphtheria, polio and measles.

Tuberculosis became less common and the immunisation programme reduced the incidence of diphtheria, polio and severe measles. Scarlet fever became less toxic, less common and rarely required admission. The wards were then used for the residential care of seriously disabled children.

Policy changes later ensured that these children were transferred to several small community bungalows. Many of the children made considerable progress in the smaller and friendlier environment. The hospital buildings were demolished and the site was used for the development of a block of retirement apartments.

Holborn Heights was a hostel for adults with learning difficulties. As with Primrose House and Green Lane, many of the residents were moved into community bungalows. The site has been sold, the buildings demolished and new housing has been built.

Sanatoria

The scourge of tuberculosis (TB) was an enormous problem and many centres were used to nurse cases in order to prevent infection spreading in the community. As tuberculosis became rare, the sanatoria either had to reinvent themselves or close.

Wrightington developed a new facility for the treatment of rheumatic disease and has become an internationally renowned centre for Hip and Hand surgery.

Greaves Hall became a geriatric centre. This too has closed, the Hall has deteriorated severely and the land has become a residential development.

Rufford New Hall became a pre-convalescent home for gynaecological patients. Some geriatrics were nursed there too. Once more, the house closed and the site sold for a new housing development.

Sefton House provided Council residential care for the elderly and is now closed. The listed building has been converted into highly desirable apartments.

Brookside Residential Care Home provides Lancashire County Council accommodation for the elderly. It is one of the few remaining Council facilities.

The Hospital that never was

The Lathom Park Estate[25] was bought by the Ministry of Health in the early 1930s. It took quite a number of years to complete the purchase. Several owners of portions of the park were unwilling to sell, and had to be taken to court for compulsory purchase orders to be made before completion was achieved. The intention was to build a very large new County Psychiatric Hospital for the treatment of acute and chronic mental illness.

There was also to be a separate large new County hospital and residential facilities for adults and children with learning difficulties. These new facilities were for the whole of Lancashire and would replace the Victorian hospitals of Rainhill, Winwick, Lancaster and Whittington.

In 1937 a new 9 inch water main was laid from Ormskirk along Crane's Lane to supply the proposed hospitals.[13i] The Ministry agreed to put out a competition for architects to design the new buildings.

Then the Second World War came, all the plans were shelved for the duration. Post War there was no money for such large capital spending.

By the time plans *could* begin again, management of mental illness and learning disabilities had changed. 'Care in the Community' became the basis of all planning. At the same time new treatments for mental illness were developed so that in-patient care was no longer required for most cases.

Rainhill, Winwick, Lancaster and Whittington are all closed and smaller units are sufficient for the needs of the County today. Most service users are treated in the community removing the need for many residential care beds.

So now we still enjoy the green park. The remains of Lathom House stables have been converted to apartments. Pilkington's built their Research Laboratory on some of the land, and the Lathom Park Chapel and Almshouses remain an isolated tranquil haven.

BIBLIOGRAPHY

1. Map of Workhouse area derived from, www.Multimap.co.uk

2. Higginbotham Peter, "The Workhouse" consulted May 2007 www.workhouses.org.uk/Ormskirk

3. Correspondence between the Principal Medical Officer of Health, John Hobbs and the Group Medical Officer, K Monsarrat, City of Liverpool, and Group Medical Officer Patrick, City of Manchester. 1939-1945 EMS files. Liverpool Medical Institution.

4. Ormskirk Union Minute Book, 1928-1930 Lancashire Record Office (hereafter LRO) PUS 1/28

5. Master's and Matron's Joint Report 1936 -1946 LRO HROR/1/1

6. Minutes of meetings of the Ormskirk Urban and District Army Social Welfare Committee 1940 – 1945 LRO UDOR/15/44

7. Unpublished diary of Lt Col SS Greaves DSO MC Commander of Hospital Ship 'Atlantis' April – June 1940 Imperial War Museum, London P172

This is a chilling account of a hospital ship facing fierce bombardment from overhead as well as from other vessels in the cold Norwegian waters off Narvik. He describes taking on board survivors from the Polish vessel 'Grom', Officers and other ranks, and of both Allied and British forces as well as POWs. He received Naval Air Arm survivors of plane crashes nearby. They told him that the Red Cross on the Atlantis was not visible from 5-6,000 feet up. This was remedied next day with the Red Cross extended to the full width of the upper deck. The ship left for Liverpool on 27th May with a full complement of 432 patients.

There was difficulty translating emergency orders and instructions into French, German and Polish, and the recording of the spelling of the Polish names was a particular problem. The last comment on that sailing was to the effect that the men with frostbitten feet could not wear boots, and that he could not afford to lose so many pairs of slippers. Those men were disembarked 'pick-a-back' without footwear.

By June 3rd, he was back off Narvik. He describes picking up a case of diphtheria and shortly afterwards a second, and a case of meningitis which he thought was probably tubercular. Again the ship suffered intense enemy action, but was itself undamaged. He returned to Scapa on June 11th and Liverpool on June 12th with a further full complement of French, German and Polish patients.

8. Medical and Surgical reports from the Medical Division of the Military Hospital, Ormskirk 1 January 1944 to 21 June 1944 National Archives (hereafter NA) War Office Papers WO/222/844

The report is signed by Lt Col Lamb RAMC, Officer in charge. He describes serious problems with amoebic dysentery, many patients suffering several relapses. There were 83 cases in 5 months. The hospital became a centre for treating it and also a centre for the clinical evaluation of newer therapies.

There were many cases of pulmonary TB and it was difficult to disperse them to suitable sanatoria. Most new cases were discharged within days.

The surgical report for same six month period states that the hospital dealt with 827 cases from the Home Forces and 137 from overseas. Of the overseas patients, 114 had disease or accident, only 23 battle wounds. The surgeon thought many of the wounded were sent to other local hospitals which meant that he could not really evaluate the sort of injuries expected from modern warfare nor could he develop suitable training for his juniors. Most of his work was normal routine surgery for hernias, eye injuries, ENT problems and simple fractures.

9. NA, DT 35/289

10. i) Lord Nuffield Provincial Hospital Trust, Survey of Lancashire Hospitals recommended by Dr Veitch MOH Manchester. NA, MH 58/327

ii) Ministry of Health Hospital Survey by Rock Carling and McIntosh, published 1945/46 NA MH 77/5

The Survey commenced in 1941, the County at Ormskirk was visited in 1942 by the authors as part of their survey in the North West.

Ormskirk, in Hospital District 7, was described as being in the Southport and South Lancashire area.

Ormskirk Voluntary Hospital. This is a small general hospital of 45 beds. There is no resident MO. Theatre and Wards poor and nurses' accommodation is unattractive. Some vacant land is available.

Ormskirk County and Institution 205beds +

There are 6 EMS huts with a peace time capacity of 156 beds since 1938.

The Maternity department has 20 beds. It is overworked and greatly in demand. There are 500-600 deliveries/year.

2 Emergency theatres (inconvenient of access) are improvised into permanent buildings. There are special emergency scheme staff. PAI has only 1 part time GP.

Ormskirk Isolation Hospital in Green Lane has 62 beds.

Conclusion This area should have its own General Hospital service.
They proposed development of new General Hospital for Ormskirk and Southport at Greaves Hall.

11. Plan of workhouse buildings adapted from Ordnance Survey 1908.

12. Robert Rawlinson, *The Ormskirk Board of Health Report 1850* reprinted with an introduction by Dr Audrey Coney, Lancashire County Books 1991

13. Annual Medical reports to Ormskirk Urban Rural District Council
    Wellcome Library, Euston Rd. London
    i) 1937 installation of new 9" water main to Lathom Park
    ii) 1940 No mention of Edge Hill or new EMS hospitals
    iii) 1943 'An ambulance has been presented by the people of Ormskirk'

14. Replica of a Casual Ward, Yorkshire Museums of Law and Order, Ripon

15. www.institutions.org.uk/asylums/england/LAN/winwick_asylum

16. Dr Pat Starkey, ed., *Nursing Memories: from probationer to professor.*
    1994, National Museums and Galleries Liverpool

17. Miss Jones, Matron to the Royal Infirmary Liverpool, Principal Matron of 22nd General Command Chester and sector Matron under the *Emergency Hospital Scheme, Correspondence and Reports of Liverpool and Regional Hospitals to the General Nursing Council 1936-1979.* NA, DT 20/131.

18. LRO, HROR/1/1 August 1940

19. NA, MH66 /889

20. NA, MH 76/243 and MH 76/247

21. NA, MH 57/217

22. NA, MH /77 1946

23. Photographs of Ormskirk houses used as POW detention centres, on display at the RAF Museum, Millom.

24. MH 95/80

25. NA, MH 67/55Lathom Park

Background reading and sources for research:-

26. M. Duggan, *Ormskirk –The making of a Modern Town*, (Sutton Publishing 1998)

27. *The Workhouse at Southwell.* The National Trust 2002

28. Trevor May, *The Victorian Workhouse* Archives, Shire Publishing 2005

29. Andy Reid, *The Union Workhouse.* British Association for Local History Phillimore and Co. 1998

30. Adrian Allan, Health Records Team, *Sources for the history of Nursing in Liverpool,* 1995 Special Collections, Liverpool University

31. Janet Foster and Julia Sheppard, *A guide to Archive Resources in the UK,* British Archives

32. *Archives on Merseyside,* A guide to Local Repositories, Merseyside Record Office

33. Special sub – committee report, *Nurses Uniforms 1936 – 7 (Chap. 2)* Liverpool City Council, Hospital and Port Health Committee, Liverpool Record Office